Dramatic Dialogue

In *Dramatic Dialogue*, Atlas and Aron develop the metaphors of drama and theatre to introduce a new way of thinking about therapeutic action and therapeutic traction. This model invites the patient's many self-states and the numerous versions of the therapist's self onto the analytic stage to dream a mutual dream and live together the past and the future, as they appear in the present moment. The book brings together the relational emphasis on multiple self-states and enactment with the Bionian conceptions of reverie and dreaming-up the patient.

The term *dramatic dialogue* originated in Ferenczi's clinical innovations and refers to the patient and therapist dramatizing and dreaming-up the full range of their multiple selves. Along with Atlas and Aron, readers will become immersed in a dramatic dialogue, which the authors elaborate and enact, using the contemporary language of multiple self-states, waking dreaming, dissociation, generative enactment, and the prospective function.

The book provides a rich description of contemporary clinical practice, illustrated with numerous clinical tales and detailed examination of clinical moments. Inspired by Bion's concept of "becoming-at-one" and "at-one-ment," the authors call for a return of the soul or spirit to psychoanalysis and the generative use of the analyst's subjectivity, including a passionate use of mind, body, and soul in the pursuit of psychoanalytic truth. *Dramatic Dialogue* will be of great interest to all psychoanalysts and psychotherapists.

Galit Atlas, Ph.D., is on the faculty of the New York University Postdoctoral Program in Psychotherapy and Psychoanalysis, and at the Four-Year Adult and National Training Programs at the National Institute for the Psychotherapies. She is the author of *The Enigma of Desire: Sex, Longing and Belonging in Psychoanalysis* (Routledge, 2015). Her *New York Times* article "A Tale of Two Twins" was the winner of a 2016 Gradiva award.

Lewis Aron, Ph.D., is the director of the New York University Postdoctoral Program in Psychotherapy and Psychoanalysis. He is the author and editor of numerous articles and books on psychotherapy and psychoanalysis, including *A Meeting of Minds*, and co-editor of the Relational Perspectives Book Series. He is well known for his study and reading groups around the world.

Relational Perspectives Book Series
Lewis Aron, Adrienne Harris, Steven Kuchuck & Eyal Rozmarin
Series Editors

The Relational Perspectives Book Series (RPBS) publishes books that grow out of or contribute to the relational tradition in contemporary psychoanalysis. The term *relational psychoanalysis* was first used by Greenberg and Mitchell[1] to bridge the traditions of interpersonal relations, as developed within interpersonal psychoanalysis, and object relations, as developed within contemporary British theory. But, under the seminal work of the late Stephen A. Mitchell, the term *relational psychoanalysis* grew and began to accrue to itself many other influences and developments. Various tributaries—interpersonal psychoanalysis, object relations theory, self-psychology, empirical infancy research, and elements of contemporary Freudian and Kleinian thought—flow into this tradition, which understands relational configurations between self and others, both real and fantasied, as the primary subject of psychoanalytic investigation.

We refer to the relational tradition, rather than to a relational school, to highlight that we are identifying a trend, a tendency within contemporary psychoanalysis, not a more formally organized or coherent school or system of beliefs. Our use of the term *relational* signifies a dimension of theory and practice that has become salient across the wide spectrum of contemporary psychoanalysis. Now under the editorial supervision of Lewis Aron, Adrienne Harris, Steven Kuchuck and Eyal Rozmarin, the RPBS originated in 1990 under the editorial eye of the late Stephen A. Mitchell. Mitchell was the most prolific and influential of the originators of the relational tradition. Committed to dialogue among psychoanalysts, he abhorred the authoritarianism that dictated adherence to a rigid set of beliefs or technical restrictions. He championed open discussion, comparative and integrative approaches, and promoted new voices across the generations.

Included in the RPBS are authors and works that come from within the relational tradition, extend and develop that tradition, as well as works that critique relational approaches or compare and contrast it with alternative points of view. The series includes our most distinguished senior psychoanalysts, along with younger contributors who bring fresh vision. A full list of titles in this series is available at https://www.routledge.com/series/LEARPBS.

1 Greenberg, J. & Mitchell, S. (1983). *Object relations in psychoanalytic theory*. Cambridge, MA: Harvard University Press.

Dramatic Dialogue

Contemporary Clinical Practice

Galit Atlas and Lewis Aron

Routledge
Taylor & Francis Group

LONDON AND NEW YORK

First published 2018
by Routledge
2 Park Square, Milton Park, Abingdon, Oxon OX14 4RN

and by Routledge
711 Third Avenue, New York, NY 10017

Routledge is an imprint of the Taylor & Francis Group, an informa business

© 2018 Galit Atlas and Lewis Aron

The right of Galit Atlas and Lewis Aron to be identified as authors of this work has been asserted by them in accordance with sections 77 and 78 of the Copyright, Designs and Patents Act 1988.

British Library Cataloguing in Publication Data
A catalogue record for this book is available from the British Library

Library of Congress Cataloging in Publication Data
Names: Atlas, Galit, author. | Aron, Lewis, author.
Title: Dramatic dialogue : contemporary clinical practice / Galit Atlas and
    Lewis Aron.
Description: Abingdon, Oxon ; New York, NY : Routledge, 2018. |
Series: Relational perspectives book series ; 97 | Includes bibliographical
    references and index.
Identifiers: LCCN 2017031441 (print) | LCCN 2017033986 (ebook) |
    ISBN 9781315150086 (Master) | ISBN 9781351368605 (Web PDF) |
    ISBN 9781351368599 (ePub) | ISBN 9781351368582
    (Mobipocket/Kindle) | ISBN 9781138555471 (hardback : alk. paper) |
    ISBN 9781138555488 (pbk. : alk. paper) | ISBN 9781315150086 (ebk)
Subjects: | MESH: Psychoanalytic Therapy—methods | Psychoanalytic
    Theory | Psychotherapeutic Processes
Classification: LCC RC506 (ebook) | LCC RC506 (print) |
    NLM WM 460.6 | DDC 616.89/17—dc23
LC record available at https://lccn.loc.gov/2017031441

ISBN: 978-1-138-55547-1 (hbk)
ISBN: 978-1-138-55548-8 (pbk)
ISBN: 978-1-315-15008-6 (ebk)

Typeset in Times New Roman
by Swales & Willis Ltd, Exeter, Devon, UK

For Shoshi and Yaakov Atlas

Contents

Acknowledgements

We would like to thank our colleagues and friends who provided their valuable feedback. Thank you, Adrienne Harris, Jessica Benjamin, Jonathan Slavin, Marie Hoffman, Meirav Roth, Melanie Suchet, Noga Ariel-Galor, and Yifat Eitan. Our gratitude to Steven Kuchuck, who edited the manuscript on behalf of the Relational Perspectives Book Series. Many thanks to Kate Hawes, Charles Bath, and the staff at Routledge. We are indebted to Ofri Cnaani for her gracious permission to use her stunning artwork on our cover.

We thank our beloved children: Benjamin, Raphi, Kirya, Emma, Yali, and Mia.

Chapter 1

Generative enactments

This chapter briefly introduces the concept of dramatic dialogue
*and sets the stage for our use of that concept by presenting several
related ideas about* enactment *and* generative enactment. *The
authors suggest that enactments are not only restrictive and repetitive, with therapeutic benefit resulting from their resolution.
Rather, enactments themselves may also be generative and growth-
enhancing. A few references to the origin and development of these
ideas in psychoanalysis provide historical context to the development of our integrative model of* dramatic dialogue.

This book emerged from the playful exchange between two voices,
sometimes merged as one, and at other times distinctly different
while remaining together in dialogue. As in the therapeutic encounter,
we are "two people playing together" (Winnicott, 1971, p. 38), and
our voices often mirror each other, merge, or split to hold dissociative
and complementary parts of ourselves. We each play a range of characters, our and each other's internal objects. As intermingled psyches
and souls, we enact our internal scenes, dreams, conflicts, and fantasies. We invite you to mingle with us, to experience and re-experience,
to feel, to love, and to hate, as we do. Following in Ferenczi's foot-
steps, we ask you to enter, with us, dramatic dialogues.

Our model of dramatic dialogues invites the patient's and analyst's many self-states onto the analytic stage to dream a mutual
dream and live together the past and the future, as they appear in the

present moment. We are at play, and metaphorically in a theatrical play, enacting and engaging in the drama of psyches in dialogue.

This book brings together the relational emphasis on enactment and multiple self-states with the post-Bionian conception of reverie, "becoming-at-one," and analysis as a co-constructed dream, as it emphasizes a regulatory system that is greater than the sum of its parts. A relational model of multiplicity lends itself to the metaphor of theater, a dramatic model in which multiple self-states, like characters, are dramatized and enacted in the transitional space of the analytic stage. This is our theater of the unconscious.

Psychoanalysis, like the writing of this book, is a collaboration, as patient and analyst dream together and, through reverie and enactment, co-create their own unique idiomatic vision and version of their inner theater. Rather than a talking cure that splits speech and action and emphasizes the analyst's inferences and interpretations, the analytic process facilitates living and re-living the psychic and relational reality of the session. This conceptualizing of dreaming and drama has, sometimes subtly and sometimes obviously, affected psychoanalytic thinking across schools and traditions in all parts of the world. Hence, a new vocabulary dominates psychoanalytic theorizing. Today's analysts speak of multiple self-states, enactment, waking dreaming, subjectivity, intersubjectivity, co-creation, and unformulated experience: a new language of psychoanalysis.[1]

Our writing reflects the changing style of psychoanalytic exposition, which follows developing trends in theory and practice. It is not surprising that such evolution would be accompanied by changes in professional communication and literature. Contemporary clinical work emphasizes the therapist's subjectivity and the patient's experience of the therapist's subjectivity (Aron, 1996; Kuchuck, 2014). Similarly, current analytic writing features the writer's subjectivity and the idiomatic use of clinical material. The author's voice is not dictatorial, narrating from a position of mastery. Authors, even individual authors, are already multiple. Resonant with challenges to the analyst's authority, the author's voices are not hegemonic. We imagine the author/analyst as a participant in an ongoing exploration of many levels of knowing and not knowing. In addition, our understanding of enactment and parallel processes includes the realization that writing enacts its content, and in that sense we deliberately invite the reader to experience a version of our realities and to live through the enacted scenes with us.

Throughout the book, and as Atlas (2016) elaborates in *The Enigma of Desire*, we use the term *therapeutic tales*, instead of speaking of cases or case presentations, in order to stress our understanding of these experiences as both subjective and inter-subjective events. To "tell a tale" has different connotations than to "present a case." Even though we received patients' permission to write and publish their stories, we treat these as fiction or narrative, as we believe our creation is a translation of the conscious and unconscious, internal and external reality, not a mirror of it. The tales we write about our patients' lives and about their minds are sketches filled with our own psychology as it is played out in the unique interaction with a specific patient. For that reason, we do not aim for a neutral presentation and instead add our personal voices and our dialogue, so as to enact the existence of two unconscious voices in the room and elaborate the zone of mutual vulnerability (Aron, 1996). This is our attempt to demonstrate through the writing itself the use of the intersubjective space, to deepen the clinical work and understanding of the unconscious.

In describing our own dramatic dialogue, we wish to evoke the spirits of Freud and Breuer (1895), who in the very first psychoanalytic book wrote about their own collaboration:

> If at some points divergent and indeed contradictory opinions are expressed, this is not to be regarded as evidence of any fluctuation in our views. It arises from the natural and justifiable differences between the opinions of two observers who are agreed upon the facts and their basic reading of them, but who are not invariably at one in their interpretations and conjectures.
>
> (pp. xxiv–xxv)

Ferenczi's clinical innovations

By the late 1920s, Ferenczi had been continuously experimenting with clinical technique for many years. He was interested in clinical outcome and clinically grounded theory rather than in abstract or removed theory. He dared to experiment with a range of clinical approaches and was encouraged in such experimentation by Freud himself, who was not averse to clinical variation so long as the findings did not challenge his major theoretical conclusions. In 1931, Ferenczi published a ground-breaking clinical paper, "Child-Analysis in the Analysis of Adults," in which he suggested that the classic approach of free association kept the patient's thoughts overly directed by consciousness and that the analyst's delivery of interpretations about these associations was not the best way to deepen the treatment. While Ferenczi himself had not practiced child analysis, he independently concluded that it was play that was the most promising vehicle for psychoanalytic transformation. He encouraged his patients to relax and played with them, referring to his procedure as the playing of games. As his experimentation unfolded and his clinical experience grew, he began to believe that the patient benefits from emotionally re-experiencing the early crucial moments of life in the presence and with the active participation of his devoted and caring psychoanalyst. Only then could the patient turn his neurotic difficulties into personality strengths and assets. As Ferenczi no longer relied exclusively on interpretation, what would substitute in its place? What would the analyst contribute if not explanations of the patient's dynamics and resistances? Ferenczi proposed that what the analyst does is enter a form of play engaging in a "dramatic dialogue" (De Forest, 1942, p. 121).

Here is the key example that Ferenczi used to illustrate his use of dramatic dialogue. A patient who had worked with Ferenczi for some time overcame profound mistrust and was trying to remember early childhood scenes. Having known the patient well, Ferenczi understood that the patient was identifying him in the transference with his grandfather:

Suddenly, in the midst of what he was saying, he threw his arm round my neck and whispered in my ear: "I say, Grandpapa, I am afraid I am going to have a baby!"

Thereupon I had what seems to me a happy inspiration: I said nothing to him for the moment about transference, etc., but retorted, in a similar whisper:

"Well, but why do you think so?"

(1931, p. 471)

In speaking to this patient, Ferenczi used the personal intimate form of the pronoun, thus dramatizing and enacting the intimate relationship in the dialogue. Ferenczi himself calls this a "game of questions and answers" (p. 471). We will show that this prototypical example has been rediscovered in their own clinical work by later analysts from many psychoanalytic schools of thought around the world, and has inspired a model of therapeutic action rooted in dramatic play and generative enactment.

Through the course of this book, we intend to rework the notion of dramatic dialogue as a model of therapeutic action and therapeutic traction. We transform the concept into a heuristic model of contemporary clinical practice that articulates how multiple self-states and internal object relations are dramatized and brought to experiential life on the analytic stage. As we will demonstrate, through generative enactments, parts of the patient come to live inside the analyst and parts of the analyst get to live inside the patient, thus the analytic encounter becomes a stage where analyst and patient come alive, working through the past and toward the future. We portray how analyst and patient learn to sustain the achievement of suffering, as this collaborative unconscious process is reflected in a two-person, relational, intersubjective context. Here we call for a return of the soul or spirit to psychoanalysis and for the generative use of the analyst's subjectivity.

In our view, and as we elaborate throughout this book, a contemporary psychoanalytic approach emphasizes experience along with insight, intuition as much as awareness, becoming rather than exclusively understanding, dreaming-up, enacting, dramatizing more than interpreting. As Bion said in his Los Angeles seminar in 1967, becoming is more significant than understanding, "because by the time you are able to give a patient an interpretation which the patient understands, all the work has been done" (Aguayo & Malin, 2013, p. 11).

The proposal that psychoanalysis proceeds through the enactment of a dramatic dialogue, rather than being understood narrowly as only "a talking cure," requires several related changes in our understanding of mind, development, and in our theory of therapeutic action, and thus we must consider some associated concepts and demonstrate their interrelatedness with the notion of dramatic dialogue. First, we will take up the idea of enactment and show how this concept has become central to so much of contemporary psychoanalysis. We propose that one function of enactment, one particularly affirmative[2] way of viewing enactments, emphasizes their constructive value, the way in which they are pregnant with future possibility. We call this dimension of enactment *generative enactment* (Aron & Atlas, 2015). Clearly, in its slant toward the future, toward giving birth to our future selves, creating our destinies, this concept already hints at the Jungian idea of a "prospective function," to which it is closely related. In the next chapter, we will examine the prospective function, reworking it within the context of generative enactment in contemporary psychoanalysis. The prospective function and generative enactment are related terms in that they both emphasize our working toward the future, in addition to our working through the past, with the analyst engaging the patient in a dramatic dialogue, a notion that we will explore in detail in Chapter 3. The mutuality that is central to the prospective function, the promising aspect of enactment that we call generative, and the dramatization that we highlight in our reworking of the notion of dramatic dialogue, are all deeply related to what Winnicott (1971) simply called play (Benjamin, 2015).

We will begin with enactment, move onto generative enactment and the prospective function, and then return to dramatic dialogue to see how these ideas convey the spirit of contemporary clinical practice. But first let's begin with a clinical tale.

Enactment

Daniel, an experienced psychoanalyst, decided to start supervision again when he felt like he was "committing a crime." He told his supervisor about Rebecca, his 38-year-old patient, who he has been seeing for the last four years.

"She is married with two young children and in fact she made a lot of progress in the years that we've seen each other."

But something bothered Daniel. More than bothered. Something haunted him.

"It's not uncommon for me to go online and Google my patients," he said with some embarrassment. "I especially like to check out new patients to see what is available about them online. But with Rebecca it feels different," he said and immediately explained. "At the end of every session I have an impulse to open Rebecca's family website and look at their pictures. It's usually late at night. I do it and I feel like a criminal, a voyeur, even a rapist. I feel that it's completely wrong but I can't stop myself."

"Do you look at these pictures from home too?" the supervisor asked.

"No. Only after our sessions," Daniel stated.

"And do you find it sexually exciting?" she asked.

"I don't think so, not necessarily. I mostly see pictures of her husband and their children, their family trips, their birthday parties."

"How did you even know about this website?" the supervisor wondered.

Daniel thought for a moment. It seems like he almost forgot how he learned about it.

"Well, I think maybe about a year ago, Rebecca started telling me about the pictures she took. She got me really interested, but I can't tell exactly how. There was something about the way she talked about it that made me curious. She is my last patient on Tuesday nights, and when she left I opened my computer and Googled her and I found that website."

Discussing this case, they suspected that the exciting and dangerous aspect was not in the content of the pictures, but that there was an enactment related to the looking itself, the fact that the therapist was secretly spying on her, invading her privacy, and that she didn't know about it. Daniel was embarrassed, and they tried to think together about the meaning of that act for this specific treatment and for Daniel himself.

But little did they know.

Enactments are powerful unconscious forces, and here they were not fully certain what was going on. In what way is this related to Rebecca's psychology? Or maybe, as the supervisor wondered, it was Daniel's form of perversion that came to the surface. But why then with this specific patient and not with others? The fact that Daniel sought supervision and was so upset by his conduct but still couldn't stop or control himself was especially concerning.

Daniel told his supervisor about his childhood and how he used to miss his mom when she was away at night, and wait for her at the window. "When I saw her walking into the building, I quickly ran into my bed and made believe I was asleep."

They wondered if looking at Rebecca's website was his way of managing his own separation anxiety at the end of the session, secretly looking at her from the window when she was leaving.

It was almost winter break, and his patient was about to take a two-week vacation. The supervisor asked him how he felt about that. Daniel said he was mostly in touch with his own need for a vacation and that he was happy he was going away with his family.

When they met again two weeks later, Daniel was shaken but also relieved. He started the session by telling his supervisor, "When Rebecca came in after the break, the first thing she told me was that her son was injured while skiing. I listened to her telling me all the details about how her son fell and how scared she was when they went to the hospital and the many decisions they had to make."

"Thank God he is fine now," she said. "I was so scared."

"And how is his leg now?" Daniel asked.

Rebecca looked at him and didn't answer. She looked confused, as if he asked something inappropriate.

"How did you know it was his leg that was broken? I never told you that," she said quietly.

Daniel paused the story for a second, looked at the supervisor and said, "Can you believe that? You can only imagine how I felt when she asked me that. I think my face was so red that I scared her. And then I just told her the truth. I told her that right before our session, I looked at her website and saw a picture of her son with a cast on his leg. I told her that I was questioning my own interest in her family pictures and I asked her how she felt about it."

Rebecca covered her face with her hands. She was silent for a long time. Daniel was silent too. He knew that she might end the treatment and never come back. He knew that he crossed a boundary, but he was also relieved that it wasn't a secret anymore.

They sat silently for a while and then Rebecca said, "Daniel, did I ever tell you about my father?"

"What do you mean?" he asked.

"When I was young, maybe 16 or 17, we found out that he used to take pictures of me and my sister in states of partial undress. Not naked exactly, but while changing our clothes and not completely dressed. My sister found a bunch of those pictures in his closet, taken as if he was outside of the bedroom watching and photographing us. We never told anyone, just took all the pictures and put them in a garbage can down the street. And we never talked about it again." She told Daniel about this family history for the first time.

This disturbing tale of what took place between Rebecca and Daniel both illustrates our thesis but also raises questions about its limits and applicability. It should be noted that like any enactment, it is hard to say precisely when it began, and perhaps we still do not know if and how it ends, mutates, or transforms. Did Rebecca begin the enactment by subtly encouraging Daniel to look at her family website? Or did he elicit information about the website because of his own separation anxiety? Who had Daniel become for Rebecca? But who had Rebecca become for Daniel? Daniel's own developmental and family history is just as essential to understanding the enactment as that of Rebecca's, whether or not Daniel's psychology is clinically necessary to discuss in her treatment.

In a strictly formal sense, Daniel did not commit an ethical violation; after all, the internet is in the public domain, and anyone can search the internet. It does not violate the law or the ethics of the profession. Still, Daniel clearly felt guilty about it as it is not in the spirit of the honesty and directness that constitutes the psychoanalytic attitude, and maybe most importantly, as he decided to not share it with her, he kept it as a secret, a sin. Nevertheless, perhaps together they were co-creating just the dance that they needed to be dancing. Perhaps they were unconsciously creating a meeting of minds, dancing to a rhythm with which they were both familiar and comfortable. Perhaps they resonated with one another just enough to enact between them precisely what had to be enacted to expose and revive a deeply disturbing memory so that it could eventually be brought to the light of day. In fact, the analysis went on with a greater vividness and aliveness. Perhaps it was Daniel's guilt and concern, his seeking consultation, and his acknowledgement with Rebecca that facilitated this happy outcome. Yet recognizing that enactment can go astray and that it has dangers does not take away from its potential therapeutic power to bring unconscious conflicts to experiential life. Let's step back now and review the development of the modern concept of enactment.

Enactment has become a widely-employed term in contemporary psychoanalysis across schools.[3] Enactment was transformed under the influence of a two-person, relational or intersubjective psychology, or what today is often spoken of as "field-theory."

Paradigmatic of the relational approach, Mitchell (1988) wrote a passage that helps analysts appreciate the value of enactment and so feel less shame in recognizing their own participation in analytic enactments:

Unless the analyst affectively enters the patient's relational matrix or, rather, discovers himself within—unless the analyst is in some sense charmed by the patient's entreaties, shaped by the patient's projections, antagonized and frustrated by the patient's defenses—the treatment is never fully engaged, and a certain depth within the analytic experience is lost.

(p. 293)

Enactments may well be a central means by which patients and analysts enter each other's inner world and discover themselves as participants within each other's psychic life, mutually constructing the relational matrix that constitutes the medium of psychoanalysis (Mitchell, 1988). Enactment speaks to the unique way in which the analyst is affectively pulled into and discovers himself or herself as a participant in the patient's relational matrix in ways that the analyst had not predicted and might not recognize until later.

Focused on the binary between repeating and enacting or remembering and verbalizing, Freud recognized those were not dichotomous processes but rather that verbal memory and behavior were equivalent, or rather transformations of each other. Hence in his essay "Remembering Repeating and Working-Through" (1914), while often contrasting remembering to repeating, ideas versus motor action, there are moments where Freud recognizes those as being different forms of memory: "as long as the patient is in the treatment he cannot escape from this compulsion to repeat; and in the end we understand that *this is his way of remembering*" (p. 150, italics added). Notice that Freud here does not say that the patient repeats to avoid remembering, but rather that repeating is his way of remembering. This is a much less dichotomous formulation, one that views these mental processes as transformations, dialectically constituting each other. This formulation opens the possibility of viewing enactment as facilitating rather than obstructing.

We begin with the assumption that patient and analyst cannot help but enact and reenact, even if in attenuated and modulated form, whatever issues are being discussed between them. "The language of speech and the language of action will be transforms of each other; that is, they will be, in musical terms, harmonic variations on the same theme" (Levenson, 1983, p. 81). Paradoxically, we also enact precisely what we are not able to put into words (Bromberg, 1998a; Davies & Frawley, 1994). Thus, we both enact what we *are* talking about, and we also enact what we *cannot yet* talk about. Enactment is not simply an overt event but an unconscious, continuously evolving, dynamically meaningful process (Gil Katz, 2013). Similarly, Grossmark (2012) described the "flow of enactive engagement" (p. 287) as the fulcrum of psychoanalytic treatment. In all treatments, a new version of the patient's early conflicts, traumas, and formative object relationships is inevitably created, without awareness or intent, in the here-and-now of the analytic dyad. Within the enacted dimension of psychoanalytic process, repressed or dissociated aspects of the patient's past are not just remembered, they are relived. Katz's (2013) contribution allows us to recognize that there is a continuously enacted dimension to all the psychoanalytic process, and that what appears to be an enactment may be better understood as a manifestation of an underlying process of change that has already occurred. In agreement with Katz, the Boston Change Process Study Group (2013) situated enactment within the larger flow of therapeutic process. Therapeutic action is viewed as part of a developmental process within the dyad that relies on implicit and emergent processes more closely tied to the body and to "relational apprehension" (p. 743)—not as a return of past dissociated memories, but rather as the threshold for the introduction of emergent ways of being, of an opening toward new relational possibilities.

The affirmative clinical attitude and enactment

Here, however, is where we hope to push our theory into new territory, or perhaps to rediscover certain trends that have not been at the forefront of the theory and bring them from the periphery to the center. The usual relational and interpersonal emphasis, following the pioneering contributions of Levenson (1983), who emphasized the explication of interpersonal patterns through the detailed inquiry, has been on resolving enactments, "getting out of enactments," questioning them, working one's way out of them, understanding them, and interpreting them. In other words, enactment is usually viewed as an unavoidable clinical phenomenon, a circumvention that is beneficial when it can be analyzed and resolved. Of course, we agree that this interpretation or unpacking is often necessary and beneficial. We are suggesting, however, that the flow of enactive engagement, the enactive dimension of analysis, may at times be fecund and transformative in and of itself, not only by working one's way out of it.[4] Our argument for generative enactment is tied to and builds on our assumption that enactments dramatize, bring to life, not only the individual's conflicts but the intersubjective field, allowing for its growth and transformation through dramatic dialogue.

Just as Freud first thought of transference as an interference with analysis and later recognized that it was what was most essential and most facilitating of analysis, so too we are suggesting that enactment was first perceived as a hindrance and was only later understood as advantageous. Similarly, just as analysts first had to learn to analyze the transference resistance and later learned to also analyze resistances to the transference, so too analysts first had to learn to analyze enactment as a mutual resistance, and only lately have they recognized that the problem may not be in the enactment but in the avoidance of enactment. Just as we speak of analyzing resistance to the transference, we need to conceptualize the analysis of mutual resistances to engaging and living out the flow of enactment.

Our forward-leaning approach to the dyadically enacted dimension of psychoanalytic relatedness, like an affirmative approach to resistance or defense (Schafer, 1983), emphasizes what the enactment is for, that is, its constructive side, rather than how it gets in the way or interferes with the process. We stress what the patient is trying to accomplish as well as what they are trying to avoid, how they are trying to grow as well as how they are trying to maintain homeostasis, how they are searching for needed relationships even while they engage in repeated relationships (Steven Stern, 2017). Notice that these are not either/or formulations. Being affirmative does not necessitate the denial of darker and more demonic aspects of life. But free of the classical limitations of drive theory, a generative approach does not focus only on the diabolical and thus avoid the developmental and growth-oriented tendencies and human strivings.

In accentuating an affirmative psychoanalytic attitude, we are drawing on a rich vein of psychoanalytic history and tradition. Considering the controversy regarding an affirmative attitude toward dreams, fantasy, symptoms, and play will shed light on our proposal for a generative attitude toward enactment. In the history of dream analysis, there have been several efforts to understand the function of dreaming in "generative" terms. Maeder, a friend of Jung's, proposed as early as 1911 that in addition to fulfilling childhood wishes, dreaming might also have the purpose of preparing the dreamer for upcoming tasks. Did dreams represent only attempts to discharge disguised childhood wishes, or "did they also sometimes have as their purpose attempts to anticipate and solve problems that lay in the near future?" (Kerr, 1993, p, 461). By 1914, the idea of a prospective interpretation of dreams and symptoms was in the air. Adler was proposing a teleological function of neurotic symptoms, and both Stekel and Adler claimed priority in suggesting the prospective function of dreams. Kerr (1993) suggested that the prospective theory of dreams was the biggest threat facing Freud in these years of defection. By 1916, Jung posited that dreams serve both compensatory and prospective functions. Fosshage (2000) suggested that dream mentation can contribute to the development of psychological organization through the creation or consolidation of a new solution or synthesis. The dream's foreshadowing of actualities that might emerge in the near future is what Jung called the prospective function, a formulation we will elaborate in the following chapter. In Fosshage's view, dreaming does not just foreshadow developments but is actively engaged in bringing about those internal changes.

In proposing that enactments result from the "interpersonalization of dissociation" and that the establishment of "relational freedom" is central to therapeutic action, Donnel Stern (2013) suggested that it is precisely because enactments "inhibit the free unfolding of the future, their resolution is one of the most important influences liberating the future to unfold more freely than the past did" (p. 232, n. 8). Whatever their differences, we join both Stern and the Boston Change Process Study Group in their emphasis on looking toward the future along with the working through of the past. Our own emphasis represents a further development of this approach in that we view enactment not only as the blockage or interference with the future, which leaves the focus only on resolving or eliminating the enactment, but rather, and as we describe in the next chapters, we imagine the dramatic dialogue of generative enactment as a rehearsal, a practicing for the future, an early effort to "work toward the future" rather than only a "working through of the past" (see Aron, 1991, p. 81).

The prospective function and a generative approach may be attributed not only to dreams but to symptoms, to play, or to fantasy. In her comprehensive survey of fantasy in psychoanalysis, Ethel Person (1995) wrote,

> Fantasy can act as a rehearsal for future action and can provide a template for life choices that may be either literal translations (enactments) or symbolic expressions of the fantasy's narrative content. Fantasy is a theatre in which we preview the possible scenarios of our life to come.
>
> (p. 6)

Person (1995) termed "generative fantasies" those that do not just repeat the past but rather focus on the future. Like make-believe and play, "generative fantasy represents a creative effort to find our way in the real world" (p. 121). It is our purpose here to suggest that just as dreams, fantasies, play, and even symptoms have been understood as generative, so too may we appreciate enactments as a creative theatrical form pregnant with possibilities. We extend Person's one-person psychological interpretation of "generative fantasies" to a relational and intersubjective formulation of "generative enactment."

Generative enactment in action

Eagle (1993) presented a case study of a young woman who had been raised by abusive parents in which there was a dramatic disappearance of the patient's chronic symptom of dyspareunia, the medical term for painful intercourse. The symptom, which is typically difficult to treat, completely and permanently disappeared following a critical episode in the therapy, which Eagle views as an enactment. At a certain moment in the analysis, Eagle had suggested to the patient that she use the couch. The patient was furious at this suggestion, but Eagle remained silent, accepting her protest without criticism, and did not interpret her angry reaction. The patient came into the next session and reported that she believed she had overreacted to his suggestion and reported that on the previous night she for the first time had sexual intercourse without pain. Only later did Eagle recognize that his suggestion that she use the couch was part of an ongoing enactment. He had suggested that she use the couch immediately after another incident. The patient had been repeatedly buttoning and unbuttoning her blouse, first one button and then two, and after observing this for some time, Eagle had pointed it out to the patient. This earlier intervention had also aroused the patient's annoyance, and here too Eagle had not intervened. But it was just after this interaction, and without conscious awareness, that Eagle had suggested to her that she use the couch. Only in retrospect did Eagle come to understand what had happened between them.

In his formulation, his patient had been testing him to see how he would stand up to various provocations. This is a woman whose childhood history had led her to anticipate that she would be punished for her incitements. Now, in therapy, she was testing her therapist to see if he would confirm or disconfirm this belief. In responding non-judgmentally to both of her protests in reaction to each of his interventions, Eagle disconfirmed her pathological expectations of being punished. He demonstrated in vivo that he did not react as her parents did, thus providing a form of corrective emotional experience, but without any conscious planning, feigning, or manipulation. The disappearance of her symptom was not accompanied by the patient's explicit insight, but rather seemed to be a function of a complex enactment in which her transference expectation was disconfirmed.

Eagle's clinical illustration of this thesis was an outstanding early example of how enactment without interpretation could lead to therapeutic progress, constituting a generative enactment. According to Eagle, there was something in the enactment itself that was curative. Eagle was caught up in something with his patient of which he was unaware at the time, and yet this jointly created, co-constructed generative enactment, without any interpretation or explication, led to the remission of a serious and persistent symptom. In fact, after the analysis was over, when Eagle asked his patient what had been most helpful, she remembered this day when he suggested the couch and did not criticize her for being angry as the turning point of her treatment.

We want to make several points about this illustration before moving on. First, sometimes a dramatic dialogue may not seem to be so dramatic. In fact, in this vignette, what Eagle stresses is what he did *not* do, rather than what he did do. He emphasizes that he "passed her tests" by not responding with criticism. But of course the interaction also included his pointing out to her that she was dressing and undressing herself, being seductive, and then immediately inviting her to lie on his couch. This invitation might have been understood as his responding to her seduction with further sexualization, or she might have heard it as a punishment that she was able to defeat with her protest. Here, it is worth underscoring that drama includes moments of silence and what seems like inactivity. A dramatic dialogue is a state of mind, not a technique, and doesn't need to involve heightened activity and interactivity.

In retrospect, Eagle himself considered his suggestion that she use the couch to have been a clinical error. We would like to suggest another outlook, and think about his suggestion to use the couch as his participation in a generative enactment, a manifestation of his unconscious recognition that there was something forward-moving in the patient's play with seductiveness and quarrelling. In our earlier illustration of Daniel and Rebecca, we suggested that Daniel unconsciously resonated not only with a trauma from Rebecca's past but with a movement toward Rebecca's future. Here too, we imagine that Eagle may have unconsciously recognized that his patient needed to seduce and quarrel with him under conditions that were ultimately safe so that she might move forward with her sexual and romantic life. We suggest that Eagle's clinical experience and expertise resided in a form of procedural knowledge where he unconsciously joined and resonated with the patient's experimentation—he joined her dance. His clinical proficiency lay in reverberating with and participating in the leading-edge, forward movement of the enactment that was generativity co-constructed.

Enactments are one of the royal roads to the fulfillment of our destinies. Building on a relational understanding of enactment, we propose that just as our interpretations employ visions of the psychic future, so too our mutual enactments anticipate or are reconstructions of the future co-constructed in dramatic dialogue. They are mini-experiments, relational trials, rehearsals, the purpose of which is to test out, modify, and refine aspects of the self's relational repertoire so as to expand relational options by finding transformational objects that facilitate the movement from fate to destiny. Enactments, and not only their interpretation or resolution, are thus a creative medium for giving psychological birth to or actualizing the self. Our unconscious participation in enactment is not only pushed or driven, determined by our history or present circumstances, but is shaped in line with our psychic futures.

Enactment is a central concept in the development of our integrative model. We invite you to travel with us from America to Latin America, to Europe and back. We will visit Freud's Vienna and Jung's Zurich, as well as Klein and Bion's Britain, Latin America, Stephen Mitchell's New York City, and Ferro's Italy, and we will meet Joyce McDougall in Paris or perhaps join her on one of her regular stays in New York. We travel in time as well. We hear voices from the past, ghosts and ancestors, and bring them to the present as we present a contemporary reading of some traditional theories.

We question the analyst's role in the intimate encounter with her patients while adding to the conversation links not only to past and present, but also a prospective function of the future, as we will describe in the next chapter.

As we bring the future to life and challenge the distinction between past and future, as well as between old and new, we will emphasize the ways in which the future of an analytic drama already lives in what we call the *prequel drama*. Through analytic tales, we elaborate on how dramatic dialogues are created unconsciously from the very first contact we have with our patients. Dramatic dialogues take place across schools of thought, across analytic cultures, as well as between patients and analysts, between writers and readers, and between co-authors. Some of these dialogues are not only across the globe but across centuries.

Mostly we invite you to listen to and participate in the enacted drama or, more accurately, to recognize that you are already participating in it, at-one with it. The writer/reader exchange forms a regulatory system, a system of mutual influence and co-creation, in which meanings emerge that are beyond the conscious intent of either alone. We invite you to our "dance party," a meeting of minds, bodies, and multiple self-states, that just as in each analytic dyad, creates a unique drama, a "generative enactment," that facilitates relational freedom (Donnel Stern, 2015). Analyst and patient not only "dream themselves into existence," to paraphrase both Ogden (2007b) and Brown (2011), co-creating the intersubjective field, but ideally join in expressive dance improvisation in which spontaneity, freedom, and expressiveness are joined dialectically with thoughtfulness, reflection, and creative choreography.

Notes

1 We are alluding here to Roy Schafer's (1976), at the time, quite radical and provocative book *A New Language of Psychoanalysis*, which called for rethinking the metapsychology, philosophical assumptions, and language of psychoanalysis. It's now almost half a century later, and our language needs ongoing revision.

2 Here too, and throughout this book, we utilize the word *affirmative* in the spirit of Roy Schafer's (1983) use of the term in *The Analytic Attitude.*

3 See Aron (1996) for a comprehensive discussion of enactment, interaction, and projective identification, as well as the interpersonalization of psychoanalysis, and Aron (2003b) for an update as the term exploded in frequency of usage.

4 Steven Stern (2017) criticizes the relational approach to enactment for its emphasis on the trailing edge of its meaning, whereas he believes that enactments can be used as part of the leading edge of the treatment. As Stern recognizes, his approach and ours have a good deal in common.

Chapter 2

The prospective function

This chapter posits that our unconscious hopes and dreams, our goals and ends, pull us toward our destiny, and highlights how we unconsciously anticipate and rehearse for that future. From objects of fate, we become agentic subjects, creators of our destiny, of our futures. Indeed, we suggest that this goal represents an additional layer of meaning to Benjamin's call, "where objects were, subjects must be." The prospective function, *an idea first introduced by Jung, does not mean* prophetic, *but rather it means that we unconsciously "look forward" to, anticipate, envision, and construct future possibilities. Two clinical tales are presented to bring the theoretical conceptualizations to life.*

We are sitting here now thinking and forming our ideas, imagining you, our future reader. When you read our words, it will be your present, and this time will be long past. And yet you are here with us now, and we are speaking to you as we write in anticipation of the future. We look back. We think about our past and the history of psychoanalysis while we are investigating the question of the future. What we write may be psychically determined, fated by our past history and present circumstances, but to the degree that we are free agents, our collaboration is also the self-realization of our dreams and destiny. We are dreaming our future, enacting and rehearsing for what is yet to come, and opening toward new relational possibilities.

Whereas traditional psychoanalysis emphasized the psychological causation driven by our past and present wishes, in this chapter we want to highlight how our unconscious hopes and dreams, our goals and ends, pull us toward our destiny and how we unconsciously anticipate and dramatically rehearse for that future. Human beings can potentially transform their fate and thus create their destiny. From objects of fate we become agentic subjects, creators of our destiny, of our futures. Indeed, we suggest that this goal represents an additional layer of meaning to Benjamin's (1998) call, "where objects were, subjects must be" (p. 29). We suggest that contemporary psychoanalysis, with its hermeneutic, constructivist, humanistic, and relational leanings, is now in a position to reevaluate the use of what Carl Jung (1916/1960), a century ago, called the *prospective function. Prospective* does not mean prophetic, or literally predictive, but rather it refers to a visionary function: We unconsciously "look forward" to future possibilities. The mind exercises or rehearses; it anticipates, prepares, shapes, and constructs. Just as Jung argued for the prospective function of dreams, so too we propose that all productions of the mind, all compromise formations, include some unconscious anticipation of the future, efforts to transform our fate into our destiny (Aron & Atlas, 2015).

Cooking a dream

Sophie, a 34-year-old successful Israeli businesswoman, started her analysis preoccupied with her future, filled with dread that she would never be able to become a mother and that "the clock is ticking, time passes too fast, and I just can't make it." Sophie begins the analysis in a state of agitation, very concrete, desperately asking again and again, "What should I do? Is anything going to change soon?" Our main focus is on her desperation and hunger. Sophie expresses her longing for a baby, while I experience her as a demanding girl who requests that I feed her as an omnipotent mother who knows everything about the past, present, and future. "What do you think, does he love me?" "What should I do? Tell me . . ." she asks again and again. I am supposed to know her future and help her to make it happen, but in my mind I hear myself echoing her: "Oh, what a hopeless treatment . . . Will anything ever change?" At that point, we are both frustrated. She has a limited ability to know her mind, use symbolic language, or play. Rather, it's as if Sophie is so hungry and empty that she has to immediately "swallow" everything I give her.

Sophie is the youngest of five children and the only girl. Her mother was excited to finally have a daughter, and Sophie admires and idealizes her mother. The mother is the one who shows restraint, who listens and knows everything. "She's God," Sophie says. Sophie's mother comes from an Orthodox Jewish home. Although her mother was religious, Sophie and her four older brothers renounced religion. "At home," she says, "no one dared rebel against mother, but everyone rebelled against God." Only the household rules remained. Mother's rules, not God's. It is not God then who knows the future, but mother, and in the transference it is her analyst.

We work in a preliminary way with Sophie's dreams (see Atlas, 2013a, 2013b, 2016). Food was the main theme in most of Sophie's dreams, and the use of dreams as a shared third enables a shift to a more playful and symbolic thinking (Aron, 2006; Benjamin, 2004; Ogden, 1994a). "We are cooking," Sophie used to call the analysis of her dreams, referring to the profound form of thinking that we shared.

One day, during the fourth year of her analysis, Sophie begins a session saying that she feels empty, that sometimes after our sessions she feels like she is vomiting water. She explains that it feels like it does after having vomited everything, when there is nothing there, she is empty, and it is painful and exhausting. She tells me the following dream: *I am in a wedding hall, where I meet an Israeli friend of mine who is a psychologist, who has come there to give a talk. I sit down at the table and see leftovers from lunch that look delicious, many dishes, and everything looks appetizing and fresh. But since I was so late, there is almost nothing left on the tables. I go over to the organizers' table, a women's table, and ask if there is more to eat. For a moment it seems to me that the girl whom I am asking is ignoring me, but a few seconds later she says, "There is no food left, but it's being taken care of [in Hebrew, "Betipul," also meaning: it's in treatment]." I say, "OK, thanks," and return to the table. But I'm impatient. I think to myself, why do I have to wait for them? It's easier to just go out and get some fast food so that I won't be hungry. I ask myself if I should trust them. It feels like I have no control. It is much simpler to buy something with my money than to wait.*

We begin by exploring the inherent question concerning whether she can trust whatever is happening in the kitchen. Since food is a main theme in this treatment, the kitchen became a metaphor for the unconscious and for the analytic process. Here the kitchen is the stage where the dramatic scene of transformation occurs. In the kitchen something is being cooked, but Sophie cannot always know what it is. "It's better to have control and go outside, to the real world and buy something with my money, the money I know I have," she says. She makes her own money and can pay for anything she needs, but she can't trust what she can't see, touch, or know. The process of waiting for the food to be cooked is too frustrating, she feels help-less, she is hungry, and she feels dependent and asks herself if she can trust the process.

There is another implicit question: Maybe *I* ate everything and left nothing for her? Maybe I took all the men, maybe I have every-thing, just like her mother. And maybe in therapy, food belongs only to me. I cook it and I serve it, and she needs to go back to her place and be patient, be a patient. Can she trust me? Can she trust herself? Can she trust the analytic process? Here she is explicitly raising these questions while presenting the option that there is something that belongs only to her. "Maybe it is not empty, maybe there is something there, in the unseen kitchen," she says. "I suddenly exist, and maybe I don't have to run and fill myself up. Maybe I am full. Maybe someone will soon fall in love with me . . ."

The following week Sophie shares another dream. She's back in the kitchen. "It's the kitchen from last week's dream," she says, "and

I see a man from afar. I don't understand what's special about him and why I notice him. He's a simple man. He touches my hand and consoles me for all of the things I have lost while riding the motorcycle with my brother [an image from an earlier dream]. I was so happy as he hugged me in front of other people and wasn't embarrassed, and I say to him, 'I love you,' and he answers, 'I know. I love you, too.' And they lived happily ever after," she jokes.

Somewhat uncannily, a day after presenting this dream in therapy, Sophie would meet the man who eventually becomes her husband. "He is a simple man," she says. "And I probably wouldn't even notice him if I didn't see him in my dream the night before. You know," she adds, "I'm sure I cooked my own food in that kitchen."

In our view, this dream, while not prophetic, was prospective, and the process itself—we believe like any other process—was looking toward and cooking the future, unconsciously preparing and procedurally rehearsing for it. The conflict between self-reliance and dependency appears in all of Sophie's dreams, as she has been exercising her sense of agency, mentally and symbolically. She was cooking and gaining a sense of mastery of the kitchen and of riding her own powerful motorcycle so that she now has the autonomy to begin to envision a romantic relationship. The dream is pregnant with the future; the Aryan origin of the prefix "gen-" in *generative*, as in *generation* or *genesis*, means "to beget." Hence the dream is forward-looking and fertile; she can cook in that kitchen without feeling that in doing so she abandons her mother or analyst.

Elaborating on Bion's alimentary model of the container/contained, Ferro (2009) used the metaphor of cooking when he defined how "emotions can be 'cooked' through their narrative transformation, with unsaturated interpretations, as the patient's response is always being 'sampled' in order to determine which ingredients are required to enrich or lighten the dish" (p. 217). In Ferro's mythic narrative, the analyst is the chef who cooks, processes raw beta elements, and transforms them into digestible form for the patient, always sampling the dish and adjusting, modulating, and regulating what is served up in the kitchen in response to the patient's unconscious feedback. In our own use of this metaphor, rather than envisioning the analyst as the cook and the patient being served up a dish, we view the analyst as inviting the patient into the kitchen itself, where the analyst and patient cook up and process the ingredients together, jointly tasting and modifying the dishes collaboratively. The process that Sophie herself called "cooking together" was a dramatic dialogue, a way of co-creating a profound form of thinking and feeling that belongs neither to patient nor analyst alone (Atlas, 2013b). Our attention is thus not limited to the outcome of the prepared dish but highlights the shared activity and process. Bion's digestive model of containment was transformed in his later writings into a sexual model of co-creativity (Brown, 2011) where mutuality and intersubjectivity are highlighted, and our approach shares that later emphasis on reciprocity. Throughout this book, we utilize dramatic dialogue as yet another metaphor, like the alimentary and the sexual, to portray the multiple scenes of therapeutic action.

Sophie was preoccupied with becoming a mother. She could not get there as long as she relied on splitting the images of baby and mother, so long as she believed that a mother must be an omnipotent god, not a dependent baby. This splitting was repeatedly enacted between Sophie and her analyst such that either she expected her analyst to be the all-powerful mother/God who provided for her, or she exerted omnipotent control over her own mind, but in a way that left her feeling both empty and unable to produce. In the process of "cooking together," oscillating and mutually enacting the functions of mother and infant, we co-created a third that transcended mother–baby oppositions and reversals. That process, as Sophie defines it, helped her to believe she is fertile, generative—that is, capable of dreaming, imagining, and producing—thus ready to become a mother. Her dreams, as they were enacted with me, were a way to dramatically rehearse for her future.

When I first asked Sophie permission to present her case material, she was proud and jokingly said that she would now become a famous actor in the analytic theater: "Do you think people will realize how amazingly my mind works? Would they see how I learned to dream my existence and make my dreams come true?" Thinking of Ferro's (2009) ideas following Bion's (1991) lines in *A Memoir of the Future*, we believe the analytic process can help our patients dream their future. Sophie believed she invited her future loving husband and the future father of her three children to her life in her dreams. Bion (1991) reminds us that our future, enigmatically, is always already ours, and that we don't remember it only for the pragmatic reason that it didn't happen yet (see Atlas, 2015, 2016). Here, linking Bion's approach with Jung's prospective function, we want to put forward the proposition that in studying the mind we need to consider the unconscious will and urge to create, envision our future, give birth to ourselves, exercise our destiny drives, and even die our own individual deaths. After all, and as Freud (1920) memorably observed, "the organism wishes to die only in its own fashion" (p. 39).

These are all conscious and unconscious processes that are based on the assumption that the mind is aimed toward mental evolution and toward the developmental capacity to bear the emotional anxiety of the confrontation with life. Whereas Freud's pleasure principle is rooted in the idea that the mind strives to avoid pain and frustration, Bion argues to the contrary that the mind develops toward transformation, to tolerate and bear pain so as to grasp Truth. Emotional growth then is about developing the tolerance for our deepest anxieties, including psychological birth and annihilation, fear of our future death and disintegration. If Freud emphasized the causality of the past, and Jung the future orientation, Bion cautioned that both the past and future can distract from the immediacy of the present, and his effort to restrict memory and desire is in the service of immediate experience. Nevertheless, preconceptions anticipate their future, and we hear in Bion's voice a trust in unconscious process and a skepticism about understanding and explanation.

Grotstein suggests that Bion not only heard Jung lecture but was deeply influenced by him.[1] Examining some of the similarities between Bion and Jung, Grotstein says, "Preconceptions, like archetypes, intuit, anticipate their future" (Culbert-Koehn, 1997, p. 29). It is this theme of the individual's effort to anticipate his or her psychic future and thus to transform fate into destiny that we will be developing. While some of the earlier theorists had conceptualized this function in terms of a one-person psychology, our assumptions weave this theme into the tapestry of the relational matrix where individuals can only fashion their destiny in an intersubjective matrix with others. This is often facilitated in psychoanalysis not only by interpreting that patient's mental conflict from the outside, but by joining the patient in a co-constructed flow of generative enactment that takes the form of dramatic dialogues. The analyst enters the field and changes the system from the inside out.

From fatedness to destiny

In spite of his complex and nonlinear views of time and causation, Freud never wavered in his natural science, deterministic principles. Freud's concept of *Nachträglichkeit*, as Lacan (1953/1956) first alerted us, is the key to his nonlinear conception of time. For Freud, the past and present mutually influence one another. Later events lead to the reworking of earlier events, affecting subsequent development. Throughout his writing, Freud depicted the mind as stratified in layers, and the analyst as archeologist, digging from the surface to the depths. However, he did not mean that memory was buried underground like an artifact preserved in its original form, waiting to be dug up. Rather, Freud viewed memory as a fluid entity that was constantly changing and being reworked over time. He referred to this dynamic as *Nachträglichkeit*, translated in English as "afterwardsness" or "deferred action," and in French as *après coup*. Faimberg (2013), in her broadening of the concept of *Nachträglichkeit*, introduced the concept of the "as-yet situation," a clinical form of temporality that includes a phase of anticipation and a phase of retrospective meaning. In illustrating her thesis, she described Winnicott as being "careful to propose an interpretation that points time's arrow toward an open future"

(p. 871). Throughout his work, Freud emphasized the determinism of the past, and yet he also recognized that all fantasy anticipates the future. He wrote, "Thus past, present and future are strung together, as it were, on the thread of the wish that runs through them" (1908, pp. 147–148), and consistent with this passage, Jacob Arlow (1986) argued that more than any other discipline, psychoanalysis sheds light on the coexistence of past, present, and future. Unconscious fantasy determines not only the anticipations of the future, but the probable modes of response to future experience. In unconscious fantasy, past, present, and future become commingled as one. As Slavin and Rahmani (2015) remind us, past and future need not be framed as binary, and the struggles, traumas, and impasses of the past can also represent "legitimate guiding forces," as Freud put it, for envisioning a different future.

Freudian theory, despite this nonlinear, complex view of time, remained deterministic, unlike Jung's use of psychological teleology. Freud's attachment to natural science determinism left no room for human agency in his metapsychology. As Caston (2011) remarked, "Matters of indeterminacy or freedom do not mix with causal determinism" (p. 910). A view of psychoanalysis as transforming passivity into activity, objects into subjects, fate into destiny, is consistent with Jung's use of teleology, referring to the psyche's purposiveness. Jung's symbolic method looks to the future and orients interpretations away from causal formulations that look back to the events of early life and to the contingencies of personal history. Jung disagreed with Freud about the nature of symbols and understood them as anticipations of new possibilities, new transformations, instead of a way backward to the past and scenes of childhood, a way forward to the psychological future. What Jung called the prospective function of the unconscious is what Deleuze, following Bergson, called the memory of the future (Semetsky, 2013). Deleuze's future-oriented epistemology is leaning toward meanings "that are yet to come" (Deleuze & Guattari, 1987, p. 5), while Freud's analytic approach was considered reductive by Jung, and then by Deleuze, because of its exclusive orientation toward the past marked by Oedipal conflict (Semetsky, 2013). Whereas Freud traced the dynamics of the psyche back to early childhood experiences, and especially to those of a sexual nature, Jung (1916) understood symbols not fundamentally as serving distortion or disguise, but rather as playing an active role in pushing the psyche forward in a development toward greater wholeness. The shift from a natural model mechanistic formulation to an existential and prospective approach posits active agents who are not simply objects of historical forces beyond their control but active subjects who shape and design their futures and whose psychic lives must always be understood as unconsciously determined attempts to take hold of their future. From our point of view, Jung's visionary teleology, unhinged from careful analysis, can lead too far from material reality, to mysticism, just as Freud's natural science approach eschews too much of psychological and spiritual life, and so we look to incorporate insights from both vertices, combining pragmatic and enigmatic registers (Atlas, 2015).

The distinction between fate and destiny is a central theme in the existential philosophy (developed in the 1950s) of Joseph Soloveitchik. For Soloveitchik (2000),[2] *fate* refers to a level of human existence in which the human being is a passive object acted upon by external forces beyond the individual's control, whereas *destiny* refers to a realm in which the person is an active subject imbuing life with meaning and significance: "Man's task in the world is to transform fate into destiny; a passive existence into an active existence" (p. 6). Note the striking similarity to Benjamin's (1998) call, "where objects were, subjects must be" (p. 29). Soloveitchik posits that it is our human obligation to partner with God in creating the world, and thus our foremost duty is to create ourselves anew. This is his understanding of *teshuvah* or repentance, to create oneself anew, but not by forgetting our past misdeeds, not by splitting them off, but rather by reworking the past in line with our present commitments. His view of time is thus quite closely consistent with Freud's understanding of *Nachträglichkeit*. Theologians have long wondered how repentance could undo past deeds, but this nonlinear view of time is the basis for solving this contradiction. Psychoanalysis, from this perspective, is a spiritual journey in which the individual works through the past to work toward a new future. The person as object becomes a subject, an agent, an author creating destiny from fate. This is the meaning of being born-again. Perhaps it is time for psychoanalysis to reclaim the psyche, the soul, as a legitimate subject of discussion?

Within contemporary psychoanalysis, Bollas (1992) posits a destiny drive, the "urge to develop the form of one's private idiom through the articulating and elaborating experiences of object usage" (p. 71). In a manner strikingly like that of Soloveitchik, Bollas posits that destiny, in contrast to fate, makes room for human agency, but fulfilling the destiny drive brings inevitable conflict because destiny calls for the determined agentic taking hold of one's future. Building on Winnicott's theory, for Bollas, to exercise one's destiny drive is to creatively make use of objects in the environment to establish one's true self. By contrast, to be passively fated by forces outside of one's control is associated with the development of a false self. "It may be an essential part of analytic work to help a patient transform fatedness into destiny and to gain futures" (Bollas, 1989, p. 44).[3] In yet another application of Winnicottian thinking, Benjamin (2015) usefully suggests that the clinical tale of Sophie illustrates the importance of the patient's activity in collaborating with the analyst as another way that mutuality and play expand the notion of the creative illusion first offered by Winnicott. Collaboration and facilitation, mutuality, is the basis of the shared third.

We now turn to self-psychological formulations that we believe have much in common with the line of thought we have been developing. We will add Kohut to the links we have been building among Jung's prospective function, Bion's memories of the future, and Bollas's destiny drive. All of these are attempts to shift from a natural science to an existential model in which human beings have the potential to transform fate into destiny, to become subjects where they had been only objects, to be existentially free agents where they had been determined by circumstance. So too the prospective approach may be linked to Kohut's suggestion that the analyst attend to the "leading edge" as well as the "trailing edge" of the patient's transference (Miller, 1985, p. 19). The leading edge addresses the evolving and developing aspects of the patient's transference, whereas the trailing edge is concerned with genetic causal configurations. The trailing edge addresses what is old and repeated, whereas the leading edge speaks to what is new. Similarly, Steven Stern (1994, 2017) focused on the importance of attending to both the needed and repeated relationship. Kohut also described the leading edge as "forward moves" (Tolpin, 2002, p. 167) and Tolpin (ibid.) called them the "growth edge" of development, and she specifically linked these ideas to a "prospective" approach. Analyzing both trailing- and forward-edge transferences, according to Tolpin, frees the patient from repeating nuclear pathology while supporting the aim of regaining developmental momentum.

The generative and prospective functions highlight that enactments are an improvised form of mutual play or dramatization that anticipate, practice, and rehearse forms of relationship and behavior looking toward the future. Enactments, from this perspective, develop and elaborate characters as a means of exploring, dramatizing, and bringing to life future potentialities, what Cooper (2000) has called, after Loewald (1962), our "psychic futures." Cooper spoke of "reconstructing the future," suggesting that in analysis "we are reconstructing both the past and, paradoxically, the future as it is represented and expressed in current interaction" (p. 15). Loewald (1962) himself demonstrated that the structure of our psyches is organized in temporal modes with the ego aligned with the present, the id with the past, and the superego and ego-ideal with the psychic future. Indeed, in the classical model, it is only with the resolution of the Oedipus complex and the consolidation of the superego that the child establishes a sense of the future, of a complex drama that leads to a psychic future in which they fulfill their place in the next generation. For Loewald, the superego represents that function of our minds that represents the past as seen from the point of view of the future.[4]

The move from the Oedipal to the post-Oedipal may be thought of as the developmental template for the transformation of fate into destiny. Davies (2003) emphasized the parent's (and analyst's) vision of the child's (and patient's) psychic future, especially in the Oedipus phase. The Oedipal parent's love for the child is an imagined sexual and erotic admiration. It envisions the child's sexual potency and charms *in the future*, and it somehow implicitly communicates this erotic idealization to the child; empowers him and "*sends him forth well prepared for the world of potential* actual sexual partners" (p. 74, emphasis added).

Davies' emphasis on the future reminds us that as early as 1946, Erik Erikson proposed that the son's resolution of his Oedipus complex was not the result of castration anxiety, but rather was best facilitated by the father's emphasis on the son's future. The clinical approach accentuating forward movement, on working toward the future as well as working through the past, is reminiscent of what Schafer (1983) has called the affirmative analytic attitude.

Elsewhere in her writings, Davies (2016) has advocated a clinical point of view remarkably like our own development of Jung's prospective function. As we previously described, Jung understood symbols not fundamentally as serving defense, distortion, or disguise, but rather as pushing the psyche forward in development. Davies was commenting on a clinical case where the therapist went along with the patient consulting another therapist, and asked whether this decision was not a form of "acting-out." Davies says that "far from 'acting out,' there was *an immanent clinical wisdom; a kind of preconscious sense of direction*" that allowed the therapist to surrender to the patient's agenda (p. 327, emphasis added). Davies is offering a viewpoint where "acting-out" is not exclusively serving defense or resistance, but is rather a developmental move forward, a force toward growth and futurity. Furthermore, we believe, and she seems to concur, that therapists need to trust their unconscious to tune into this prospective function of behaviors, symptoms, symbols, and transference manifestations, to join in, participate, and play with them, thus transforming them into generative enactments.

Enactment as a rehearsal for the future

Sarah has been complaining about her marriage since she began her analysis 7 years ago. She came to treatment suffering from bodily pain, pain in her knees that interfered with walking, and pain in her elbows. She believed that her physical condition was in some way related to the pain she felt in her 12 years of marriage, pain caused by feeling that she was not heard by and could not get through to her husband, even though he was a "good guy." At night she tried to avoid him, and moved to sleep with her 3-year-old son, while her husband stayed alone in their bedroom.

Sarah felt much safer when sleeping with her son. She felt close to him and loved. She said she was afraid of the end, but the end of what? The end of her marriage? The end of her analysis? The end of her life?

As a child, Sarah was a popular girl with many friends, and later in adolescence she had several boyfriends, but felt that no one really knew her and that if they did, they would not like her because there was something bad hidden inside of her. Sarah was always told that she was a beautiful child, and in fact was regarded by others as a beautiful woman, but she never thought of herself as either popular or attractive; rather, she believed her beauty hid her internal ugliness, perhaps in the same way that she believed her parents' advanced education disguised their ignorance. Sarah's father was a judge in a state court. Both parents were highly educated, economically and socially successful, but they were morally rigid, emphasizing strict standards of right and wrong, and were unable to tolerate the expression of affect. Sarah herself knew that it was "right" to keep her marriage. She knew her parents wouldn't accept any other behavior. She knew it was "wrong" to express so much dissatisfaction and agony.

Sarah decided to start therapy when her joint pain became insufferable. She tells me that she is afraid she is about to become paralyzed, that she is worried about her future. As the years went on, Sarah became increasingly clear about her feelings of dissatisfaction and was better able to articulate her concerns. Sarah would at times become convinced that her husband, Josh, like her mother, was dissociative, incapable of expressing or even identifying feelings, was depriving, punishing, and could never join in her feeling states. But neither of us was convinced that this was what he was really like. In fact, it was confusing since we both knew Josh was also protective, stable, solid, often encouraging her to do what she most desired, and genuinely believed that they had a good-enough marriage. Josh was committed to her as his wife and the mother of his child, so that he thought that in her ongoing complaints she was somewhat hysterical and overly dramatic, exaggerating the problems between them. I joined in her confusion. To what extent were her perceptions related to her childhood experiences, we wondered, noting the parallel of her past and present convictions as she also felt her parents were solidly there and committed to family and yet she did not really believe they loved her.

Very often in the course of dramatizing Sarah's relational world we switched roles, where I played Sarah and she played her husband's part; Sarah would come to the sessions on time, worked hard, paid promptly, and yet like my patient in her marriage, I felt that something was missing. I sensed that there was something we were still unable to touch, as if there was no ability to think about what was actually happening inside and outside the analysis. Thinking and affect started and ended with her intolerable pain. As I started to recognize my own inability to think, I became more aware of the ways her insights and introspection were used masochistically in the service of guilt and stasis. Sarah began treatment blaming herself and quickly moved to explore the many reasons she felt at fault for her marital discontent. There was a thin line between Sarah's insight and her self-recrimination in the service of not being able to move, physically because of her joint pain, and emotionally, as she was trapped in the masochistic position. She, and we, were paralyzed.

Focused on her pain, I was trying to grasp any vision she or I could have of her future. The future seemed empty. There was no imaginary scenario of what she would like to have inside or outside of her analysis, inside or outside of her marriage, no fantasy of creating something new with her husband or with me, not even a forbidden fantasy of being with another man, who could perhaps love her the way she needed. At times, I felt that her mind attacked all linking (Bion, 1959), between objects, ideas, affects, images, different aspects of her personality and of our interaction. These attacks on linking kept her fragmented, disjointed, and unable to dream or think, and therefore unable to move, incapable of transformation, of learning from experience (Bion, 1959, 1962a).[5]

In the room with Sarah, my own reverie included life filled with light, children, music, food . . . and sexual thoughts, which Sarah asserted she certainly didn't need. I wondered if my reveries of abundance were only a way to keep myself alive with her, to soothe the pain, and in what way they were connected to her process, in what way I was dreaming her life, my life, and our future. I think about reverie as belonging not only to me, but as part of a shared process, existing within the intersubjective field. Rather than understanding reverie as the product of an isolated mind, detached from the patient, we frame reverie as a co-created dramatic scene and assume a flow of unconscious communication between patient and analyst and linking them together.[6] I realized that I dreamt a future, and as I started to silently connect my reverie with a potential for a full life, Sarah notified me that she was ending her analysis. Sarah didn't want to discuss or process that decision, and I was left with the feeling that maybe I dreamt something she had to attack, cut off, so that no transformation would occur. I did not yet know that our enactment was a step forward for both of us and not only a repetition of destructive attacks and paralysis. Thinking along more conventional lines, I inferred that quitting the treatment was a defensive displacement, namely that she was cutting me off as she wanted to cut off her husband because she still couldn't face the catastrophe of ending her marriage; instead, she ended her analysis. To some degree, I could think of the analysis as repeating the deadness and hopelessness of her marriage and of myself as a participant in those dynamics. One question that I asked myself was whether Sarah's unwillingness to discuss these considerations with me might have been related to some reciprocal conflict or avoidance on my own part. Could it be that there was some relief for me in her leaving because her marital struggle was too close to my own? All of these reflections and considerations emerge in an attempt to search for the repetition of old object relations, and in that respect these repetitions need to be uncovered and processed. Alternatively, we suggest that at times what seem like mutually engaged old scenarios, the trailing edge, may turn out, from a different vertex, to be new developments in the process of transformation, a leading edge of development. There is always more ambiguity and multiplicity of meanings than we can ever know or consciously articulate. Sometimes, and perhaps often, only the future can teach us about the meanings of the past.

Six months later, Sarah calls me. She asks to resume her analysis. "I left," she says, and as I am about to acknowledge her wish to return to treatment, she adds, "I don't mean the analysis. I left him. Right after I ended the analysis, I left Josh."

Years later, we came to understand her interruption of the analysis as an enactment. She left the analysis not only as a defense or resistance but rather as a way of rehearsing for her future, a preparation for the end, for leaving her marriage and starting a new life, with new love, hopes, and dreams. Enactment, as we have noted, is a process rather than a discrete episode, and so here one might question whether Sarah's interruption was itself an enactment or whether it is better viewed as the end of what had been a sado-masochistic enactment between the two of us that preceded it. The flow of enactment is continuous.

The clinical understanding that we are proposing in this chapter is that the disruption of the analysis was not only defensive but adaptive and constructive in at least some respects, and this is the register that we have called generative enactment. In interrupting the analysis, Sarah took an initial step in a move from passivity and paralysis to activity and decisiveness. There was a gradual transformation from someone who could not dream, who had to express herself concretely by attacking her joints, her links, attacks that kept her from knowing and having an emotional experience for which she did not feel prepared. She slowly developed the ability to use her mind, make connections, and imagine her future. She used her analyst's mind to transform her night terrors into a dream with connections, with joints that could move, so that she could think and symbolize (see Ogden, 2005). The enactment was also a way to transform an experience of masochistic submission into agency and self-authorization, from being disjointed to feeling connected, and so she slowly transformed her life experience from fate to destiny.

We consider the option that this generative enactment was not only a rehearsal for Sarah's future but that Sarah and I co-created a dramatic dialogue in which we enacted our similar and different hopes, possibilities, and potential future. As we described in the previous chapter, in contrast to the term *acting-out*, which emerged within the context of a one-person psychology, the concept of enactment, as it has been developed and elaborated since the 1980s, is embedded within a two-person or bidirectional model (for the historical development, see Aron, 1996). We believe that enactments are co-constructed even at times when it might superficially look as if one person is "acting-out." The analyst is always a participant in the unconscious drama shaping the patient's future, but the assumption that we can always come to know the analyst's contribution is of course an illusion. The analyst's unconscious is no less complex than the patient's, and so our focus is on those things that we cannot fully know, or that we cannot know at all. In this case, while eschewing any sense of certainty or mastery of the analyst's unconscious, we can play with the idea that it was the analyst's reverie, which was an expression of the analyst dreaming her patient's as well as her own life, that contributed to the enactment of a jointly constructed treatment interruption, perhaps even including as one component the analyst's unconscious wish to get rid of the patient who "has no future." In sum, what seem like impasses, disruptions, stalemates, gridlock, even interruptions may at another time, from a different perspective, look more like progress and transformation.

Whereas much of the contemporary literature has considered the analysis of enactments, the explication of these repetitive patterns, "getting out" of enactments, and resolving impasses and stalemates by understanding and explaining them to all be therapeutic, we are suggesting another approach, conceptualizing in another register. As mentioned in Chapter 1, we believe that there is much we may never be able to understand about what happened in an enactment, but that the enactment itself, and not only its resolution, may be a dimension of a transformative process. Enactments, like anything else between patient and analyst, can be restrictive, limiting, and destructive, or may be expansive, growth-promoting, and creative. The analyst therefore must straddle a paradox, always skeptical, questioning, seeking hidden meanings, searching for unconscious dynamics at play, the trailing edge, a hermeneutics of suspicion, while also, and paradoxically, trusting unconscious process, seeking the leading edge, and surrendering to the continuous flow of the enactive dimension of analysis, relying on a hermeneutics of faith (Ricoeur, 1970), and searching for what is generative and progressive.

We cannot discuss Sarah's endings and the future without noting the too-often neglected and denied role of anticipating death (Razinsky, 2013). When discussing the unknown and the future, we tend to forget that there is one thing that is certain in everyone's future, and that is our death. We want to be explicit in linking the prospective function and the anticipation of the future with the significance and denial of death in the psyche. We will expand on this connection elsewhere, but for now our suggestion is that it is tempting to work with what we assume we know, the past that already happened, the patient's history, while it is more challenging to think of enactment as anticipating an uncertain future, a future that may be filled with promise and hope, but that also inevitably entails pain and loss. As Bollas (1989) suggested, we repress not only our past but our future. Thus the prospective function contains the light and the dark, hope and dread (Mitchell, 1993). Recognizing and containing our ignorance of both of the analyst's and the patient's futures is an important aspect of the mutual vulnerability that is an ethos of psychoanalytic praxis (Aron, 2016).

In conclusion, we suggest that it is essential for us as clinicians to take an affirmative approach to our patients' presentations, which are to be understood in at least one register as their best effort to develop their psychic futures. One aspect of such an approach is to think prospectively as well as retrospectively, searching for genera as well as for trauma, since both are necessary, as to think only prospectively would neglect causation and repetition, might promote the denial of aggression and conflict, and would encourage a naïve optimism and utopianism. We must consider both what enactment avoids, defends against, and repeats, its trailing edge, the repeated dimension of the relationship, as well as what it is for, what it accomplishes, and how it prepares us for our future, its leading edge or the needed relationship. Just as we may "get stuck" in enactments, unable to work our way out of them, so too we may inhibit or avoid entering into or surrendering to therapeutically generative enactments. At times, we may prematurely interpret our way out of enactments that would have been better off further lived through and elaborated in analytic play. That was precisely the intention of Ferenczi's radical innovation of dramatic dialogue, which we will elaborate in the next chapter. Just as we need to see how as analysts we participate in being used as both old and new objects, so too, and as a very important part of such a view, enactments both repeat and work through the past and anticipate, rehearse, and work toward the future, toward the transformation from fatedness to destiny.

Notes

1 It is well beyond the scope of this chapter to elaborate on Jung's influence on contemporary relational and object relational schools of psychoanalysis; however, suffice it to say that it is profound and remains largely unrecognized. Bion and Winnicott were each influenced by Jung and contemporary Jungians. They actively participated in a group with Michael Fordham, who was a founding member and chair of the first society of analytical psychology in London. This group met regularly beginning in the 1940s, under the auspices of the medical section of the British Psychological Society, and included both Winnicott and Bion as well as their colleagues Clifford Scott and John Rickman. The areas of influence are numerous, but for our purposes here we would highlight

Jung's view of the Self as containing the tension of opposites, both/and, as well as the transcendent function, which together anticipates recent intersubjective work on "the third" and multiple self-states. Clearly, this topic demands further scholarly elaboration.

2 Rabbi Joseph B. Soloveitchik was the towering genius of American Jewish orthodoxy, Talmud and philosophy, in the 20th century. It should be noted that Soloveitchik's book cited here, the English title of which is *Fate and Destiny* (in Hebrew, *Kol Dodi Dofek*), was originally given as a lecture in 1956.

3 For recent studies of agency within psychoanalysis, and especially those emphasizing the development of agency through the negotiation of recognition and mutuality, see especially Caston (2011), Gentile (2010), Hoffman (2006), Pollock and Slavin (1998), and Slavin and Rahmani (2015).

4 As Leavy (1989) clarified, Loewald's view of time, following Heidegger, is not linear or objective time but rather psychic time, "in which past and future are at work in the present, the past by reminiscence, the future by anticipation" (p. 238). Compare Loewald's approach to temporality with our earlier discussion of Freud's *Nachträglichkeit*.

5 In our perspective, which draws on Bionian and relational models, her "joint pain" expressed both intrapsychic attacks within her mind and jointly shared interpersonal pain.

6 In his *Clinical Diary*, Ferenczi (1932) referred to "Dialogues of the Unconscious" (p. 109), and wrote, "Ultimately I meant by this that when two people converse, not only a conscious dialogue takes place, but an unconscious one, from both sides. In other words, next to the attention-cathected conversation, or parallel to it, a relaxed dialogue is also pursued" (p. 84). For a clear exposition of Ferenczi's divergence from Freud regarding unconscious communication and its relation to contemporary relational theory and psychoanalytic practice, see Bass (2015).

Chapter 3

Dramatic dialogues

This chapter develops the book's central idea of dramatic dialogue by presenting its history and development as a model for understanding the therapeutic action and the therapeutic traction of psychoanalysis across numerous schools of psychoanalytic thought. Dramatic or dramaturgic models have always been two-person or field-theory models that framed therapeutic action in terms of staging and enacting the internal and relational world. In our usage, dramatic dialogue is not a prescription or form of technical rationality, but rather a model that acknowledges the inevitable participation of analyst and patient in co-creating, co-directing, and co-starring in an emotional and relational drama.

Having traced in our first chapter the concept of enactment and generative enactment, and in our second chapter the idea of the prospective function, in this third chapter we will discuss the history and development of the idea of dramatic dialogue as a model for understanding the therapeutic action and the therapeutic traction of psychoanalysis, and trace its discovery and rediscovery across various diverse schools of psychoanalytic thought. Our contemporary view emphasizes dramatic dialogue as a way of conceptualizing the therapeutic encounter rather than as a prescription for analytic technique, or what is so often today referred to as a "manualized treatment."

Our use of the term *dramatic dialogue* is but one of several metaphors that we will use in this book to capture changing conceptions of therapeutic action. Dramatic dialogue, unconscious dialogue, dreaming together, cooking together in the analytic kitchen, the analytic dance party—these are all metaphors that are meant to symbolize the patient and analyst constituting a new system. This system is something bigger than each individual alone or together. It has emergent properties that are above and beyond the two individuals that make up the analytic dyad, and as we elaborate in Chapter 7, is a regulatory field constituted by self- and mutual regulation, where each individual is a part of, and at-one-with, attuned to, the larger system. Implicit in these metaphors is something beyond words, beyond interpretation, beyond the intrapsychic; something is changed in the field that is communicated and enacted unconsciously. In this chapter, we will cover a lot of territory to provide a historical tour of how some of these concepts have developed in a variety of analytic schools and traditions.

There have been many analytic theorists and traditions that have drawn on metaphors of dramatization and theatrics, both before and after the term *enactment* was popularized in the mid-1980s. Whereas enactment emerged from within a model that featured interpretation as the primary intervention of the analyst, dramaturgic models have always been two-person models or field-theory models that framed therapeutic action less in terms of insight alone and more in terms of staging and enacting the internal and relational world. In our usage, dramatic dialogue is not a technique but rather a model that acknowledges the inevitable participation of analyst and patient in co-creating, co-directing, and co-starring in an emotional and relational drama. While recognizing dramatic dialogue as an inherent dimension of the analytic encounter has its clinical implications, we would like to underscore that our intention is to open a way of thinking about analytic processes and conceptualizing the model of therapeutic action, rather than to encourage analysts to act or enact with their patients. Throughout this book, we weave together the idea of enactment and dramatization with the notion of dreaming together, dreaming up the session. An implication of this position, as Benjamin (2015) suggests, is that dreaming and enactment, when grasped in their positive affirmative form, might be more similar, more entwined than heretofore seen, that enactment can be a way, as Bromberg (2006) recommends, of "bringing in the dreamer." Enactment and symbolization are not opposing forces, as was conventionally thought, but rather interact and interdigitate, forming a third, a "transcendent function" that might be best captured in the metaphors of drama and dreaming (Aron, 2000; Jung, 1916/1960; Samuels, 1985).

Description is not prescription

In an early and important article that serves as a prequel to the relational perspective, Greenberg (1981) suggested that referring to the analyst's participation is a description rather than a prescription. He contended that psychoanalytic technique is often presented in the imperative mode, as an injunction, a prescription, and he persuasively argued that we would be better off describing analytic process rather than prescribing. Our account of dramatic or unconscious dialogues is another way of describing what analysts and patients do with each other and is not yet another prescription for analytic technique. As Greenberg (2001) went on to assert, "there is no technical posture the analyst can adopt that will guarantee the creation of a predictable atmosphere in the analysis" (p. 362). Bromberg (1994) agrees, writing,

> Any attempt to turn a therapeutic discovery that emerges from a relational context into a technique that can be "applied" to other patients is an illustration of what I believe to be the single most ubiquitous failing in all analytic schools of thought as methods of therapy, and the shared blind-spot in each of their creators (including Freud, Ferenczi, Sullivan, and Kohut).
>
> (p. 541)

Relational psychoanalysis was thus founded on the premise that understanding, rather than prescriptive technique, was essential to the psychoanalytic method.

We will begin our examination by reviewing the history of the dramatic dialogue between Freud and his colleagues Ferenczi and Jung and travel in time and geography with Bion, Searles, McDougall, Mitchell, Grotstein, Ferro, and Bleger. In this and in the following chapters we will elaborate and develop the concept of unconscious dramatic dialogue along our own lines, in our personal idiom, illustrating its application with numerous clinical tales, both from our practices and drawn from across the wide range of psychoanalytic literature.

Sándor Ferenczi: psychoanalysis as play

After many years of clinical practice treating the most difficult cases, those who had often been dismissed as unanalyzable, and after decades of being Sigmund Freud's closest friend and collaborator, Sándor Ferenczi gradually developed his own clinical approach to psychoanalysis that was in many ways different from Freud's. Ferenczi was critical that Freud's technique and relations to patients were overly intellectualized and distant, even unfeeling, dismissive, and hypocritical. Ferenczi's critique would by the early 1930s be most sharply aimed at his friend, teacher, and analyst, Freud, but even earlier, this disputation had been directed toward the mainstream of psychoanalysis, the Berlin school, typified by Abraham and Sachs. By 1924, together with his friend Otto Rank, Ferenczi launched a major critique of the Berlin school. Already in their monograph *The Development of Psychoanalysis* we find a comprehensive critical appraisal of what had become standard psychoanalysis. Ferenczi and Rank emphasized that intellectual understanding was insufficient and that patients had to re-experience their significant historical relations in the immediacy of the here-and-now with the analyst. (For a range of perspectives on the rediscovery of Ferenczi, see Aron & Harris, 1993; Harris & Kuchuck, 2015.)

Whereas Freud emphasized turning repetition into remembering, Ferenczi and Rank suggested that the repetition of early relationships with the analyst was itself transformative. Indeed, this was not contrary to Freud, but simply a shift in emphasis, as Freud too had noted that repetition could be the patient's way of remembering.

Nevertheless, for Freud the ultimate healing agent was remembering rather than repetition, whereas Ferenczi and Rank saw value in the repetition itself, that is, in the enactment with the analyst. In contemporary psychoanalysis, we are more interested in holding the tension between insight and enactment. In this book, we will connect the contemporary understanding of mutual enactment as a means of therapeutic action with Ferenczi's understanding of dramatic dialogue.

Rather than a didactic or educational, intellectualized, or remote form of participation, Ferenczi's dramatic dialogue did not rely on passive explanations along the lines of a teacher and a student, which was his view of Freud's procedure. Ferenczi would enter a form of play, a dramatic type of game, in which at times the analyst might express his own natural feelings and emotional reactions. This, he believed, might draw out the expression of more feeling from the patient. In exploring both the patient's personal characteristics and the mutual relationship, Ferenczi believed this method maintained a highly charged tension for optimal analytic work, an atmosphere that replicated the intimacy of the parent–child relationship.

Ferenczi (1931) tells us that some patients objected to his calling this approach a game "play-analysis" (p. 472), because it seemed to diminish the seriousness of their process. It is typical of Ferenczi that he did not deny the significance of this accusation, but rather acknowledged that even while advocating the advantages of play, he also had to recognize how it could be used to trivialize the significance of the dialogue. Furthermore, Ferenczi acknowledges that it humbles him to yield so much of his professional authority to recognize that he often must follow his patient's lead in this dramatization. And finally, according to Ferenczi, this dramatic play leads both patient and analyst into altered states of consciousness, twilight states, regressed or primitive modes of thought, and these dissociated trance-states facilitate enactment and reenactment, particularly of traumatic scenes. Ferenczi values these enactments as essential to the treatment.[1] Thus, Ferenczi's dramatic dialogue is from the first associated with a lessening of distance and remote authority, learning from and valuing child analysis and play, emphasizing mutuality, recognizing trauma, enactment, and multiple self-states.

In his *Clinical Diary* (1932), Ferenczi passionately argues, contra Freud, for the therapeutic necessity of dramatization. The passage is cited by Lothane (2010) to highlight Ferenczi as an interpersonalist and dramatologist:

> to take seriously the *role* one assumes . . . that is actually to transpose oneself with the patient into that period in the past (a practice for which Freud reproached me for, as being not permissible) . . . [According to Freud,] we are dishonest if we allow the events to be acted dramatically and even participate in the drama. But if we adopt this view, and continue right from the beginning to present the events as memory images that are unreal in the present, he may well follow our line of thought but will remain on the intellectual level, without ever attaining a level of conviction.
>
> (pp. 24–25; emphasis is Ferenczi's)

In our reading, Ferenczi was not suggesting that analysts artificially play a role; in fact, he was quite critical of insincerity. Rather, Ferenczi believed that the analyst's genuine feelings would naturally and spontaneously lend themselves to this form of dramatic dialogue. Similarly, as we are at pains to repeat for emphasis, our intention is not to present a pragmatic instruction, but rather a model of therapeutic action, a theoretical way of listening to the analytic encounter and conceptualizing analytic process. Although talking about therapeutic action, we are not thinking in terms of "technique" with its prescriptive, linear, and impersonal connotations.

Clara Thompson and Izette de Forest

At this point in our narrative, we will examine an important debate between two highly significant female analysts, both patients and students of Ferenczi: Clara Thompson and Izette de Forest. Thompson, a colleague of Sullivan and Fromm, was the key figure in taking their two approaches and blending them with her own approach, significantly influenced by her analysis with Ferenczi, and creating what became interpersonal psychoanalysis.[2] Izette de Forest trained with Ferenczi directly both in Budapest and during his stay in New York. Not only was she analyzed by him, but she also did three control cases under his supervision and received a certificate from Ferenczi as a psychoanalyst.[3] These two analysts, close friends, engaged in a heated or, one might say, dramatic debate, regarding their perspectives on Ferenczi's clinical approach. Because of Clara Thompson's dominance within mainstream interpersonal psycho-analysis, it was her perspective that became most influential in that circle. Only following the discovery of Ferenczi's late work has there also been a recent rediscovery of de Forest's work and inter-pretation of Ferenczi.[4]

The dialogue and debate between Thompson and de Forest directly concerns many of the central clinical questions that we will be raising in this book concerning the advantages and dangers of Ferenczi's clinical approach, dramatic dialogue. De Forest captured the essence of what she took to be Ferenczi's clinical attitude in her (1954) title *The Leaven of Love*. Thompson was generally more critical of Ferenczi than de Forest, and believed that Ferenczi con-fused the idea of giving patients all the love they *need* with giving them all the love they *demand*. De Forest believed that Ferenczi only advocated giving them the love they needed. A contemporary analyst will recognize that the topic of differentiating a wish and a need has been a central theme of debate for the past few decades and that it reverberates with questions of technique, analytic love, and the difference between developmental arrest and conflict models of psychopathology (see especially Mitchell, 1991a, and Ghent, 2002).

Thompson voiced the opinion that Ferenczi was so concerned with being the good loving object that he did not address aggression sufficiently. Thompson knew that Ferenczi had corrected himself toward the end of his life and no longer attempted to feign a loving attitude, but she continued to disagree with de Forest about the need for the analyst to affirm or verbalize their love for the patient.

Thompson objected to Ferenczi's play technique, to what de Forest calls, summarizing Ferenczi's clinical approach, "dramatic dialogue."

The phrase *dramatic dialogue* links together in one concept speech and action such that patient and analyst are co-participants in talking with each other and interacting with each other, understanding that both are always intertwined (see Harris & Aron, 1997). Thompson was concerned that this approach, closely related to what we today call "enactment" (the dramatic reliving with patients of their traumatic past), while sometimes valuable, could also be dangerous for patients, or retraumatizing. Of course, it is critical to remind ourselves that while today many of us take enactment for granted as inevitable, this was not at all the case at the time that Thompson was writing, when it was believed that the analyst, an expert in human relations, could avoid participation in such reenactments. In short, Thompson felt that Ferenczi's (and, following him, de Forest's) advocacy of analytic love left out the necessary and direct probing of the patient's aggression, while simultaneously his search for early childhood trauma encouraged excessive regression with which the patient could attack and manipulate the analyst.

We believe that there is truth on both sides of this debate. On one hand, Ferenczi was clearly someone who longed to be loved and appreciated. He desperately wanted to be a "good object." But at the same time, he struggled with this tendency, recognizing it in himself. He thus built into his approach the acknowledgment that ruptures were inevitable, that try as he might, with all conscious intent, he would nevertheless inevitably retraumatize the patient and be drawn into the role of the "bad object." Ferenczi maintained the hope that when this happened, he would own up to it with honesty and genuine remorse. Looking back at the debate, it seems that de Forest did not sufficiently appreciate the inevitability of becoming the traumatizing object, while Thompson did not quite recognize that Ferenczi acknowledged this inevitability.

These key clinical questions and debates remain at the heart of current discussions in our field: The usefulness and dangers of regression, the role of direct confrontation versus empathy, the importance of early developmental trauma and its reconstruction, the place of analytic love, the centrality of interpretation versus experience, enactment and play, and the nature of the analyst as not only a "good" but as a "bad" object. These are the very questions that were raised by Ferenczi himself and debated by his followers and students.

We should briefly mention a third woman, and perhaps the most important source, of Ferenczi's late clinical contributions, namely Elizabeth Severn. De Forest, Thompson, and Severn were all patients of Ferenczi's in his later years. All three became transmitters of his legacy.[5] Severn (1933/2017) describes the development of *dramatic dialogue* in her mutual analysis with Ferenczi. It was a clinical innovation "that enables the patient to relive, as though it were *now*, the traumatic events of his past, *aided by the dramatic participation of the analyst*" (p. 72, emphasis added).

Fire in the theater

From the very beginning of the history of psychoanalysis, dramatization and theatrical performance played a powerful role in the emergence of theory and practice. Psychoanalysis and psychotherapy have their origin in Joseph Breuer's (1893) famous case of Anna O. (Bertha Pappenheim) treated in 1880–1882 when she was just past 21 years of age. This "talking cure" was a treatment consisting of the telling of stories: "She at once joined in and began to paint some situation or tell some story" (p. 29). Breuer noted that Pappenheim[6] was markedly intelligent and had poetic and imaginative gifts. It was she who described her psychotherapy as the "talking cure," "chimney sweeping," and referred to her free associations as her "private theatre." Not coincidentally, both Breuer and Pappenheim loved the theater, that is, the professional theater of real actors and actresses, and they were inclined to take the lessons of theater seriously. There was much talk at the time of "catharsis," an Aristotelian idea popularized by Jacob Bernays (Freud's wife's uncle) in the 1880s. Both Breuer and Pappenheim were interested in and influenced by the lessons of the stage, of theatrical performance. The "cathartic method," as Freud and Breuer (1895) called it, had its direct origins in the study of theater and tragic drama.

In his paper "Observations on Transference-Love" (1915b), Freud writes that in erotic transference, "There is a complete change of scene; it is as though some piece of make-believe had been stopped by the sudden irruption of reality—as when, for instance, a cry of fire is raised during a theatrical performance" (p. 162). In Freud's analytic theater, there is a division between those who are on the stage (the patient) and those who are in the audience (therapist). It is only when there is a fire (erotic fire) that the scene shifts, reality breaks in, and the show must stop before analyst and patient burn together, as fire doesn't differentiate between those on stage and those in the audience. Interestingly, that division between stage and audience existed in Freud's self-analysis as well, and this was later institutionalized as the split between the observing and experiencing egos. In contrast, Jung's approach to his confrontation with the unconscious emphasized play and active imagination, including the active imagining of what we are calling here dramatic dialogues. A comparison of Freud's and Jung's approaches to their self-analyses will illuminate the nature of their internal divisions, conflicts, and splits.

Freud's and Jung's self-analyses

Freud's method of self-analysis was overwhelmingly textual. He (as the analysand) wrote out his dreams carefully and then approached the text as an objective outsider (the analyst). His analysis of his dreams was systematic, meaning that he broke them up into small units and associated to each. He then wrote a good deal of the analysis in letters to Fliess, and both doctors discussed the "patient's" unconscious. While Freud is playful, his play had to do with words and cleverness in elaborating associations. It is distinctly adult verbal play.

Although Jung too was deeply immersed in literature and developed his ideas mostly while surrounded by his library, nevertheless his method was playful in the sense of his returning to childlike play, and he created an active dialogue between the "patient" and the "healer" inside of him. Jung wasn't only the wise analyst; he was simultaneously a child and an adult, as he described, "he had no choice but to return to [his childhood] and take up once more that child's life with his childhood games" (1961, p. 118). Jung described this development as a turning point, realizing that to re-establish contact with his childhood self, he had to play the games that he played as a child. While waiting for patients, he would play with stones, building with them as he did in his childhood. His valuing of childhood play anticipates the work of the developmental psychologist Piaget (who was analyzed by Jung's patient Sabina Spielrein), and of the psychoanalyst and pediatrician Winnicott.

Jung worked not only on his dreams but also on his vivid fantasies and visions. He transcribed them carefully but also illustrated them, and these became the basis for his *Liber Novus* (*The Red Book*), the decisive record of his ongoing self-analysis. Jung became convinced that the unconscious was autonomous, a force that was beyond him, not-me, and that its internal figures, archetypes, or what later would be viewed as "internal objects," were filled with wisdom and superior insight from whom he could learn. Philemon, a gnostic figure, became a sort of guru to him, a teacher from whom he could learn. He learned to trust the wisdom of his unconscious, and so he talked with its inhabitants. Jung's method of "active imagination" consisted in transforming ideas into images, concretizing his inner fantasy figures, elaborating them playfully and artistically, and entering imaginative and dramatic dialogues with them. In his self-analysis, Jung did not just transcribe his fantasies and dreams but rather reworked them, illustrated them, engaged them in conversation.

The theaters on the couch

Among analytic writers who have utilized the metaphors of theater was Joyce McDougall, a brilliant analyst, author, and supervisor who was herself elegant and dramatic, capturing the attention of those in any room she entered. McDougall wrote two books that used theatrical metaphors: *Theaters of the Mind* (1985) and its sequel, *Theaters of the Body* (1989). McDougall elaborates a theory of psychoanalysis as enacting a drama, in which the mind's "I" plays out, enacts on the psychoanalytic stage, its hidden dramas along with the accompanying scenarios and characters that make up the psychic repertory. McDougall's view of the mind is that it contains multiple internal objects or multiple selves, although that language was not yet in vogue. She begins her prologue, "The Psychic Theater and the Psychoanalytic Stage," with a quote from Raymond Devos, a French comedian: "One always hopes to become someone only to find out in the end that one is several" (McDougall, 1985, p. 3).

It is essential to see that the metaphor of enacting one's private theater on the psychoanalytic stage requires a model of the mind as made up of multiple self-states or characters, an internal universe of characters, parts of ourselves, many different people who all claim to be I. Our scripts were written when we were children and are naïve and childlike, and this child self struggles to survive in a world whose dramatic conventions are far different from that of the child. According to McDougall, our psychic scripts are enacted both in the theaters of our own minds as well as in the theaters of our bodies, and they are also enacted in the external world, sometimes using other people's minds and bodies, or even using social institutions, as their stage. We use others as stand-ins to play out the problems of the past, reproducing the same tragedies and comedies again and again.

McDougall compared her notion of the psychoanalytic stage to Winnicott's ideas about transitional space, the intermediate area of experiencing that lies between fantasy and reality, the place of cultural experience and creativity. As psychoanalysis unfolds, the patient's inner characters slowly emerge on the psychoanalytic stage: "All jostle to be heard, understood, possibly applauded" (1985, p. 14). People from the patient's present-day life join the crowd of characters as do the important figures of childhood; parents, siblings, family characters, even past generations play their role in the human drama, bringing the various scripts to life. The analyst, in this view, stands in for the people who make up the patient's private theater, even while she recognized that the analyst's own inner characters and secret scenarios might play a role in the analytic discourse, in what we are calling the dramatic dialogue.

For McDougall, psychoanalysis was always a form of liberation. She quotes Sartre as a motto for the work of analysis: "If you want your characters to live, then liberate them!"[7]

Dramatology

The word *drama* is derived from the Greek root *dram-*, "to act," and the essence of drama is action, dialogue, and emotion. Lothane (2009, 2011) introduced the term *dramatology* to emphasize that people primarily perform their emotions and experiences and only secondarily chronicle these as narratives. From the perspective of the psychoanalytic method, *dramatic* and *dramatology* mean live dialogue in the here-and-now. In those interactions, patient and analyst are drawn into conscious and unconscious enactments, which take both by surprise but offer considerable therapeutic value. Through the notion of generative enactment, with which we began our book, we start thinking about those dramatic dialogues that exist in an analytic exchange and their implications for contemporary practice.

Historically, psychoanalysts have predominantly worked with the ideational content of the person's internal world of thought and fantasy, that is, with their free associations as the primary data. They tended to see the patient as a narrator rather than as an actor and interactor. Similarly, the analyst was viewed as relying predominantly on interpretation, also narration rather than action, hence the inevitability of a one-person psychology that downplayed interaction, the dramatic. Interestingly, in a careful study of the original German texts, Lothane demonstrates that when Breuer and Freud spoke of the patient enacting or acting-out, they were using the German term that in its era clearly connoted dramatic enacting on a stage. Patient and analyst engage their dynamics as live performance. Lothane views dramatology as a necessary consequence of a two-person psychology in that the dyadic is dramatic! The most important finding of the interpersonal approach is that the meaning of a symptom, or action, is embedded in the interpersonal context, that is, what does the symptom do to the other, what kind of response does it elicit?

We think here of Stephen Mitchell's (1986, p. 124) frequent use of the Sullivanian term "gambit," in that all the patient's behavior, all that the patient presents to the analyst, is viewed as a strategy to create a precise interpersonal integration, an invitation for the analyst to respond in some way that will achieve a specific form of interaction. Rather than understand transference, or any illusion, such as idealization, as simply a form of defense or as a developmental striving, Mitchell views the patient's presentation as an invitation to a specific form of interpersonal interaction, an invitation to the analyst to dance in the patient's steps, that is, to enter a dramatic dialogue. In Chapter 5, we will return to Mitchell's dance metaphor, considering contemporary developments in psychoanalysis and particularly our own approach of dramatic dialogue.

The drama of the field: Bleger's dramatic point of view

Latin American psychoanalysis, unlike American ego psychology, was never an exclusively one-person psychology but always had an emphasis on the two-person or relational field. The individual's internal drama was viewed as being played out in the external relationship with others, including the analyst, as pointed out by Gabbard (2012) in his discussion of Latin American psychoanalysis. This led to an emphasis on the dialectic between internal and external and a recognition that patient and analyst exerted mutual influence on each other. José Bleger (1969/2012) called on psychoanalysis to adopt a "dramatic" point of view and contrasted this dramatic viewpoint with the traditional, dynamic point of view:

> Dramatics is an understanding of human beings and their behavior in terms of events that refer to the very life of human beings considered as such, whereas dynamics attempt to reduce dramatics to an interplay of forces, to such an extent that from a theoretical point of view these forces and instincts dominate and even determine human events.

> (p. 996)

Bleger continued to explain the difference between the dynamic and dramatic point of view by suggesting that "in the case of dramatics it is human beings with their human characteristics, life and behavior, whereas in the case of dynamics it is forces and instincts" (p. 996). The dynamic point of view is "unipolar," a one-person psychology, whereas the dramatic point of view "implies that phenomena are never unipersonal but bipersonal or relational" (p. 998). In sum, for Bleger, the classical dynamic point of view lines up with naturalistic science, objectivity, a "unipersonal" or one-person psychology, whereas the dramatic point of view is associated with the human sciences, a two-person psychology, relational, or bi-personal field theory. Bleger's dramatic point of view is inherently interactive. Dramatics are configured and expressed within an interpersonal field. There are no associations that are radically removed from action, just as there can be no interpretation that is only a verbal communication and not also an action. In Chapter 5, we will take up Ferro and the post-Bionian field theorists, but here we have highlighted how the Latin American analysts developed an approach that bridges many of the schools more familiar to English-speaking readers with an emphasis on a dramatic or dramatological approach.

In these first three chapters, we have spelled out the notions of generative enactment, the prospective function, and dramatic dialogues as core themes that we build on to capture the essence of contemporary clinical psychoanalytic practice. One of the goals of our project is to argue that this understanding of therapeutic action is common among otherwise disparate psychoanalytic schools and cultures. Our use of generative enactment and dramatic dialogue highlights our vision of psychoanalysis as an intimate conversation on multiple levels of consciousness, in which it is not energic forces that are studied, as much as characters and personifications of self-states and object-relations in symbolic and pre-symbolic, Enigmatic and Pragmatic, verbal and nonverbal registers, a person point of view in contrast to a mechanical model.

Throughout this book, we make use of a wide range of analytic theorists and writers. We have read these authors over many years, and they have roles in our own dramatic dialogue. We are inspired by these figures and evoke their spirits as we attempt to give them voices as characters on our own analytic stage while we dramatize our understanding of contemporary psychoanalysis.

We would like to end this chapter with an emphasis on dramatic dialogue as a clinical concept like Stanislavski's description of good theater as working from inside outward, which designates the difference between "seeming and being" (1963, p.61). Stanislavski's emphasis on "being" is crucial to our understanding of the inevitable drama that is at the heart of the therapeutic encounter, where the therapist doesn't try to act "as if" she is the object, but becomes that object.

Notes

1 The multiple self-states of the patient are also played out in the body with various body parts, such as fingers or hands, signifying a variety of the patient's dissociated self-states.

2 Sullivan himself had considered his own contribution to be interpersonal psychiatry and not specifically psychoanalysis. But by blending Sullivan with Fromm, who despite his criticisms of Freud nevertheless considered himself to be Freudian, and mixing in the influence of Ferenczi, it was Clara Thompson who birthed interpersonal psychoanalysis as a psychoanalytic school of thought. Interestingly, it is often the two men who are cited as the major theorists, but they did not always see eye to eye and might not have viewed themselves in any way as constituting a unified school of thought. It was a woman, Clara, who accomplished that unifying achievement.

3 Nevertheless, not being a medical doctor, she was not acceptable to the American psychoanalysis of her time or affiliated with a psychoanalytic institute, and so she worked on the margins. Yet, as Brennan (2009) has shown, it was de Forest who was the first to describe Ferenczi's clinical approach at a time when he too was unacceptable to the orthodox analytic community.

4 To understand just how intertwined and dramatic the relationship was between Clara and Izette, consider that both were analyzed by Ferenczi, both came back to the United States and were later analyzed by Fromm (with whom they also became lifelong friends), and both of Izette's

children were later analyzed by Clara! Fromm would go on to become one of Ferenczi's greatest defenders following Jones's dismissal of him as psychotic, and undoubtedly Fromm's understanding of Ferenczi was influenced by his analytic work with these two former patients and students of Ferenczi's (see Brennan, 2009).

5 Severn's (1933/2017) *The Discovery of the Self* has recently been republished and Peter Rudnytsky's introduction to the new edition provides critical historical information about the often contentious and rivalrous relations among these women.

6 Pappenheim would later go on to become the founder of professional social work, the founder of the League of Jewish Women, an author of both social criticism and of children's stories, as well as a translator, and a fighter struggling with women's oppression. She was the daughter of orthodox Jewish parents who educated her in the values of *Bildung*, culture and self-improvement, which emphasized literature, Goethe and Schiller, as a way to enter mainstream society.

7 Aron (2014) described one illustration of McDougall's style in her supervision of one of his early analytic cases. For a period of about a year, the patient, Al, so took for granted that Aron was homosexual that he told his friends he had a gay analyst. Then Al ran into Aron on the street when he was walking hand in hand with his wife, and the patient was shocked to see that his analyst was with a woman. Interestingly, when Aron told Joyce McDougall about this incident and questioned her about how she might handle it, she suggested that Aron tell the patient something along the following lines: "Oh, I would just say, forget that you saw me with her, how unfortunate that reality has entered the picture, go right back to believing that I am homosexual and forget what you saw. All we care about is your fantasy world, not about reality!" This was quite typical of McDougall in being creative, dramatic, playful, and focusing exclusively on psychic reality over material reality.

Chapter 4

Therapeutic action and therapeutic traction

The clinical tale of Anna is presented to illustrate and open a discussion of the notions of dramatic dialogue and generative enactment. Drama, as well as a sense of futurity and history, has been traditionally understood in terms of the Oedipus complex. This chapter develops the relationship between multiple self-states and the dramatic point of view—the elaboration of characters on the analytic stage. Several clinical examples from the work of the relational analyst Stephen Mitchell are used to show how what he called "clinical outbursts" can be usefully understood in terms of generative enactment and dramatic dialogue.

Anna is upset with Oliver. He was lying in bed again, seeming depressed and disconnected. She came home and he hardly said hello but instead turned his back to her and went back to his computer. "I can't stand him anymore," she says. "He is a depressed loser and I'm stuck with him."

When I started seeing Anna, about 5 years ago, I wondered why she didn't leave Oliver or do anything to change the dynamics that bothered her so much. They were together for many years but never got married or had children, although both of them wanted to. Somehow, that didn't happen. Somehow, he became more and more cut off and depressed, and she became more and more angry and verbally abusive toward him. They were both stuck in an unsatisfying relationship.

Anna's parents were the perfect couple. I was aware that I started envying them right from the beginning of the treatment, when Anna described how her dad wakes her mom with a kiss every morning, how he makes her coffee and then they sit in the kitchen and analyze their dreams, giggling and planning their day. Anna, their eldest daughter, was never part of that ritual and always hoped that one day she would find a husband just like her father. In her therapy, for the first time, she got in touch with how excluded she felt (just like the way she felt when Oliver was on his computer or preoccupied with himself). Abundance belonged to the parental couple, and she could only hope she would be able to create that for herself one day. She was lonely and constantly failed at being the "right girl."

This triangular dynamic developed into the drama of an ongoing narcissistic injury and rejection, a drama of envy and self-hate, and a drama of mother and daughter; where the mother "has it all" and the daughter wishes that one day she, too, will have something for herself. Days turned into years, and the hope for a better future is the only thing Anna is left with. "One day I will have," is her internal narrative, and in the transference I become the mother she loves and wishes she could one day be.

On that particular day, Anna is especially upset. "I can't stand him anymore," she says. "He is a depressed loser and I'm stuck with him." I listen to her and know that Oliver is not only the one who rejects her, but that over the years he also became experienced by her as a disowned part of herself: the loser that she hates. The winners and the losers are important characters in her internal drama. She always hoped to win and somehow ended up losing. And she hates Oliver for not being her father, for not helping her become her mother. She hates him for his vulnerability and flaws. As in every relationship, projections and introjection are powerful forces, and it isn't clear what belongs to whom anymore. I listen to Anna and feel how hurt, angry, and devastated she is. I feel sorry for Oliver, who I understand also represents the weak and attacked part of herself, and I ask, "What do you think, why is Oliver so depressed?"

"He has a good reason," she answers. "He just failed a very big test at work," she says dismissively.

"He failed," I note.

"Yes, he is really miserable," she says. "I actually feel bad for him. But still, what the fuck? He should be nice to me!"

"Yes, because otherwise you feel so bad about yourself and get really, really angry and you want to kill him," I say.

Anna nods her head. "Yes, I want to kill him. And I hate that I become that person."

"You hate him for making you hate yourself," I note. "You hate him for being a loser like you," I hear myself adding and immediately want to take my words back. "Where did that come from?" I ask myself. "Why am I so aggressive? Telling her she wants to kill him, stating that she is a loser. Am I only pointing at the obvious projective piece here, or am I becoming as abusive as she is to Oliver? Did I try to protect Oliver? To protect that attacked part of Anna that is projected onto Oliver? Or maybe I'm trying to protect myself, because I feel like a loser, not being able to help her change anything for 5 years. What kind of a therapist am I?" I hear myself thinking this as I'm looking at her, anxiously waiting for her response.

"I wish I were you," Anna says decisively.

"I wish *I* were me," I answer immediately.

"But you *are* you!" she says, annoyed.

"Are you sure?" I answer.

"Come on," she answers right away, "you are everything. You are smart and compassionate, and if you were there with Oliver in bed, you would know exactly what to say to make him feel better and to calm yourself down."

We are both silent for a moment, and I make up my mind to not interpret the transference and the splitting as I usually do, but instead to just keep our dialogue alive. "That person that you are describing," I say seriously, "I really hate her. She knows everything that I don't know. She is smart and insightful and she can actually make everything work. I bet her life is so well put together, and you know what? I'm not joking, I really don't like her. Like you, I wish I were her."

Idealization is a mechanism so powerful in its relentless push for expression that I trust that when one needs it, even bringing it to a patient's awareness often only contributes to, rather than diminishes, the idealization. For Anna, the idealization of her mother was a way to strive for contact with her idealized self, and to cover up her envy and the hate that she was so afraid of. There is a part of her that hopes I will be the one in bed with her as her sexual partner, and that through making love I will love her, merge with her, and give her everything her parents and Oliver can't. She invites me to be the one in bed with Oliver, sometimes with her and sometimes instead of her, but she also hates me for that, and hates herself for not being able to become that person she imagines I am.

Anna looks at me quietly and says with a smile, "I guess both of us hate her. No matter how much I try, I always fail." She holds her face with her hands and then whispers, "Why did you use the word 'kill', before? What made you think that?" We are both silent and tears fill Anna's eyes. "I want to tell you something—I don't know why I was never able to share this with you before." Anna tells me that she tried to commit suicide when she was 16 years old. "They took me to the hospital and saved my life. After a few days I went back home, and we never talked about it again. I never told anyone outside of my family about that."

I feel my heart beat, and Anna continues, "You know, I always hoped that if I spent enough years with you, I would become you, and wouldn't want to kill myself anymore. Instead I found out that I wanted to kill everyone, including you."

Let's consider this therapeutic tale in terms of multiplicity and co-creation, along with what we have been calling dramatic dialogue and generative enactment. In fact, this story raises a fundamental question about the therapeutic action of psychoanalysis. We have a startling example of a shift in a patient's state of mind, not just a momentary alteration but a significant structural transformation of her mind. Until now, Anna was never able to tell the analyst about her suicidal history and, more importantly, she herself had not had such clear and direct access to her own suicidal state of mind. Something happened between patient and analyst that led to a significant change that allowed the analysis to move forward and deepen. The pertinent question is, what happened here? How do we conceptualize therapeutic action? How do we achieve therapeutic traction?

Let's begin with multiplicity. We have already noted the multiplicity of Anna's states of mind. Something about her own suicidal and homicidal thoughts and actions had been split off, dissociated, or disavowed. Even as she had never "forgotten" about her suicidality, nevertheless she had, by never discussing it, stripped it of personal importance. She had kept it less organized, less developed, less well-formulated than she might have (Donnel Stern, 1997). In Freudian terms, she had deprived it of a certain type of significance, disconnecting its meaning from its significance. This is how we understand Freud's (1894, 1896) two dazzling papers on the neuro-psychosis of defense where he traces neuroses to a split between ideas and affects. Ideas provide meaning, and affects contribute the felt significance. Freud shows that the basic unit of mind is the idea linked with the affect, meaning with significance. Pathology then results from the splitting of this basic unit of mind. This is indeed what Freud meant by repression, whether or not a memory had been literally forgotten.

Very often, Freud's fundamental idea of repression is misunderstood or simplified, and it is often thought that by *repression* he meant *forgetting*. While forgetting is one possibility, what is more critical is to understand that repression expresses itself in trivialization. A memory is deprived of significance and is therefore trivialized, made to feel inconsequential. Anna had always remembered her suicide attempt; it was never forgotten, nor was it purposefully kept as a secret from her analyst. It simply had never come up because it had never felt significant or relevant. This is precisely what Freud meant by repression, but which is often referred to these days as dissociation. In this clinical tale, it was the analyst who reconnected the meaning to the affective significance by expressing the murderous fantasy with strong feeling and intensity. It was the therapist who here enacted the aggression, not as an outside observer but as an active participant in an emotional drama. Had the therapist interpreted the murderousness directly, it might well have mobilized defenses, but by enacting the aggression the patient could more readily identify with the feeling at some distance and thus reconnect the meaning and significance. It was the analyst's speaking as a character in a dramatic dialogue that facilitated therapeutic traction.

One sees here just how important linking and attacks on linking were in Freud's early work—which, of course, brings us to Bion.[1] Bion would probably point to Anna's inability to Think, when thinking holds both cognitive and emotional processes and the relation between the two. What can help one to think, then, and how does our contemporary theory frame the analyst's mind as part of that process of Thinking?

When discussing multiplicity, what stands out in this tale is the analyst's multiple self-states and her analytic use of these states. Among the very first things that the analyst tells us about herself is that from the very beginning of the treatment, she felt envy that her patient's parents were such a perfect couple. This openness to her own experience already expresses a certain useful form of multiplicity, of observing herself, taking into account her own experience as an object of the patient's usage so that she maintains a subjective and objective sense of herself without splitting the two apart (Bach, 1998).

Later, in revealing to Anna how she could envy herself—"I wish I were her too"—the analyst models what Bollas (1989, pp. 64–67) has called a "dialectics of difference": I can be multiple, at least conflicted if not altogether beside myself. I can disagree with myself, dislike myself, argue with myself, hate myself, and so you too may gradually disagree with me, argue with me and hate me, and furthermore you can come to accept and even value that you can disagree with yourself, hate or envy yourself, and be of more than one mind about things. Through this "interpersonalization of dissociation" (Donnel Stern, 2004, p. 213), the analyst co-creates a transitional space that allows the patient to eventually "stand in the spaces" (Bromberg, 1998a) or achieve thirdness (Aron, 2006; Benjamin, 2004).

These enactments, these interpersonalizations of dissociation, may begin, as Bromberg argues, with either the patient or the analyst; either way, it is always a two-way street, a mutual and reciprocal process. We would add here that when we discuss Searles in a later chapter, we will see in further detail how his view of multiplicity, multiple self-states in himself and in his patients, is often illustrated and connected to states of envy of his patient's inner objects and of his own. In his historically early utilization of multiple-self theory, Searles wrote evocatively of his own jealousy of the various characters with whom his patients were engaged. He was jealous of their relations with internal objects and could also be envious and jealous of the Harold Searles with whom they were engaged in their idealizations. Not only with patients but even with his students and colleagues, he described how many of them expressed that they wish they could be as competent and as clinically extraordinary as Searles. Searles responded that he too wishes he could be that Harold Searles. He could deeply identify with their wish to be him, since he too wished he could be himself. The notion of multiplicity thus necessitates a focus on such psychoanalytic fundamentals as splitting, introjection and projection, jealousy, envy, and problems of identity and identification.

It is often claimed that relational analysts, and for that matter contemporary analysts generally, downplay the Oedipus complex, as Loewald (1979) captured in the title of his classic "The Waning of the Oedipus Complex." It is therefore noteworthy that in this case, as well as in many others illustrating this book, the Oedipus complex plays a central role. Anna may struggle with envy and hatred that some might consider more primitive than Oedipal, as it is mixed with splitting and earlier defenses. But in our view, pre-Oedipal and Oedipal dynamics are always condensed and are never traceable to some linear line of development (Aron, 1995; Atlas, 2015). The Oedipus complex is particularly relevant and poignant for our thesis because the very nature of the dramatic is in and of itself Oedipal in nature. In the pre-Oedipal universe, there is frustration and gratification encountered in a dyadic structure: "I want from you, and you either give me or you don't." That is not dramatic. It is only with the structure of multiplicity, thirdness, that the primal scene becomes a dramatic scene: "I want and you will not give me because of your relation to another. Now I have to compete with another and overcome your commitment to them to get what I want from you." Envy here becomes triadic jealousy, and we shift from multiple part selves or self-states to the relations among multiple separate subjects. Here, we do not think of these changes as divided in terms of diagnostic categories or by linear developmental lines; rather, both dyadic and triangular relations go on simultaneously in different registers as seen from multiple vertices.

Indeed, the Oedipus is particularly significant for our thesis because it not only ushers in triangularity, rivalry, competition, and a sense of the dramatic, but even more critically it is with the Oedipus that the child begins to have a sense of futurity. From a contemporary point of view, both genders can say:

"One day I will have all that my mother has."
"One day I will have a husband like my father."

What is important here is not only the content of wanting whatever it is that she wants, but the structure of a future in which she begins to imagine herself later in life. Triangular fantasies, when not bogged down or derailed by neurosis, are the primal exemplars of generative fantasy. The Oedipus is a multi-character drama that includes rivalry and jealousy among whole objects, meaning among like subjects, and it includes a sense of the future, in health, of turning fate into destiny.

A first reading of this tale may give the impression that the analyst was simply caught up in the acting out of her countertransference, and that is certainly one view of the case. But we would emphasize a very different vision. We have already described how we view the analyst as having modeled a certain acceptance of her own multiplicity and of standing in the spaces among her multiple selves. We want to add another angle.

Mitchell (1988) describes how analysts finds themselves caught up as co-participants in passionate dramas. Sometimes he discovered that the best way out of an impasse was through an outburst. As we will see shortly, by "an outburst" he did not mean a conniption or impulsive blow-up, but rather a therapeutic intervention in which analysts used themselves fully, emotionally, and intimately. In the case of Anna, we suggest that the analyst, highly attuned to Anna and identified with her more deeply than what was traditionally called a "trial identification," was acting out of her vision of the patient's future. The analyst's engagement with Anna was steered by the prospective function, that is, by a sense of where the patient was going, by a sense of direction or purposefulness. The analyst's impression was largely unconscious, improvised, and spontaneous but was rooted in careful disciplined observation and many hours of listening to Anna. We suggest that just as patients have a prospective function that guides them toward their own future and destiny, so too do analysts utilize a trained and refined prospective function that attunes them to a sense of movement, direction, and futurity. When Mitchell called for an outburst, we believe that what he was getting at was a way in which the analyst challenged a sense of stasis by directing the patient forward, shaking up the system to generate therapeutic action and therapeutic traction. We are thus emphasizing the generative function of enactment. This is precisely what we demonstrated in the cases presented in Chapter 2.

Stephen Mitchell's clinical outbursts

Let us consider several clinical vignettes from the work of Stephen A. Mitchell that illustrate how Mitchell entered into dramatic dialogues with his patients rather than offering interpretations from a supposedly neutral analytic perch.[2] Among Mitchell's most influential writings is the chapter called "Penelope's Loom" in *Relational Concepts in Psychoanalysis* (1988). In it, Mitchell described his work with Sam, a depressed man from a despondent family, in a longstanding involvement with a downhearted woman whom he wanted to leave but could not. Mitchell described Sam's family of origin in detail and, of course, told these stories masterfully and humorously. Sam was drawn to people who suffered and with whom he could be empathic and helpful but then would feel ensnared. He felt closest to people when he could cry with them. Describing his own experience as Sam's analyst, Mitchell alternated between his enjoyment of the cozy atmosphere and surrendering to Sam's deeply sensitive, warmly sympathetic presence and attentive ministrations, and Mitchell's own powerful resistances to that pull, which were characterized by detachment and manic reversals.

One day, Sam came in to a session feeling good after an exciting success. As it happened, Mitchell tells us, on that day Mitchell himself felt depressed. With hawk-like acuity, Sam perceived Mitchell's dejection and felt horrified that he had allowed himself to feel elated in the presence of another's suffering. This seemed to Sam like a barbaric crime, and he immediately plunged himself into a depressive state.

Mitchell struggled with himself. Should he interpret Sam's feelings of guilt, his loss of an attachment to a depressive other; should he interpret Sam's enactments in reverse of old self/object relations, a form of manic defense? Or might these interpretations just reinforce and perpetuate Sam's guilty, depressive self-recriminations? Mitchell felt caught between joining Sam in his serious depressive integration or resisting it with manic reversals. He had to find a way to break out of this binary trap, to imaginatively find a way that was neither joining the melancholy nor simply reacting in a manic flight; he had to demonstrate and act another way, using his imaginative capacity, interpersonal flexibility, and reflexive awareness to create options.

Mitchell reached the same conclusion that Ferenczi had when he realized that interpretation alone was not the answer. Ferenczi suggested that the analyst enter a dramatic dialogue with the patient, meaning to enact the various "characters" that make up the patient's internal world. The analyst, as discussed in Chapter 3, enters the patient's psychic theater and plays it out on the analytic stage in a way that is spontaneous, authentic, improvised, and affectively present. Mitchell put it much the same way, writing, "the analyst discovers himself a co-actor in a passionate drama . . ." (1988, p. 295). In this case, Mitchell tells us,

> The analyst asked him in that session whether it had occurred to him that the analyst might not resent his good mood, but might actually feel cheered by Sam's enthusiasm and vitality (which was in fact the case that day).
>
> (p. 304)

It had never occurred to Sam that he could be attached and connected to others in any way other than through his depression and suffering.

Mitchell did not comment on, or about, Sam's inner world; rather, he entered into it in a personal way that touched Sam and showed him new options in living.

Here is another case example. John sought treatment with Mitchell as part of a campaign of self-perfection (Mitchell, 1988). Mitchell wrote pages delineating the defensive and adaptive functions of John's grandiosity, but he tells us that his central technical problem was how to position himself vis-à-vis John's grandiosity. To confront or interpret the grandiosity as defensive would have either driven John out of treatment or led to a submissive defeated withdrawal. To allow his grandiose claims to stand would not provide any therapeutic traction. Mitchell found a third course of action:

> What seemed most useful was a playful participation in and appreciation of John's grandiose claims, combined with an inquiry into their origins and functions . . . Sympathizing with his despair at a business failure, while noting that what was at stake apparently was not just the business venture itself but his role in the evolutionary development of the species, proved useful, as did comparisons between his relation to his company, and Louis XIV's relation to the state.
>
> (p. 218)

Note that here, too, Mitchell believed that interpretation alone was insufficient and certainly that the traditional interpretation of dynamics from an outside seemingly objective perspective would not be useful. Instead, Mitchell intervenes personally and with humor, creativity, and teasing playfulness. In one of his many memorable passages, Mitchell wrote,

> I do not propose going to the dance and complaining about the music, but enjoying the dance as offered, together with questioning the singularity of the style . . . Most analysands need to feel that their own dance style is appreciated in order to be open to expanding their repertoire.
>
> (p. 212)

Mitchell was of course using dance as a metaphor, but we believe that this metaphor is carefully chosen and reflects Mitchell's attitude toward the analyst's clinical stance and function. Mitchell views his task as to "dance" with the patient on the analytic stage, to engage actively and personally, to try out new moves, to take new steps, to feel the music and respond authentically and with personal improvisation. This is not traditional interpretation in which the analyst provides an explanation of the workings of the patient's mind as an outside observer; rather, he enters a verbal dialogue in which the patient and the analyst dance together, attuned to each other, to the music and rhythm, and adjust their steps with reciprocity and direct engagement (Knoblauch, 2000; Ringstrom, 2001).

Joining the dance was among Mitchell's favorite and most influential clinical metaphors (perhaps a tennis match being a close second). Those of us who worked closely with him were all influenced in our clinical work by this lively and playful image. In retrospect, however, there was something too simple about the metaphor. It could convey the impression of a conscious and deliberate process on the part of the analyst, who supposedly might know what steps needed to be introduced or taught to the patient so as to expand the patient's repertoire of dance steps. The analyst would join and enjoy the dance, but was also the teacher–observer who could determine what dance steps should be taught next, what steps were missing, and how next to elaborate the dance. There was something linear, educational, and consciously planned about that image. Remember, however, that this allegory was developed and articulated in 1988, before Mitchell began to elaborate his model of multiple self-states. We believe that our description of the "dance party," which we will describe in our last chapter, fits a psychoanalytic model of multiple self-states and the enactment of complex object relations, and especially emphasizes the mutual unconscious participation of both the patient and the analyst in all of their multiplicity. It leaves us with Mitchell's clinical spirit but with less of a linear and consciously directed form of analytic participation.

Mitchell first introduced the idea of the Self as relational, multiple, and discontinuous in 1991 and elaborated it further in 1993, and although it ushered in an important new focus for relational psychoanalysis, Mitchell was clear from the start that a view of the self as multiple was deeply rooted in American interpersonal psychoanalysis. Mitchell traced the idea especially to Harry Stack Sullivan, who emphasized the self as manifold with his conception of "me–you" patterns. Sullivan believed that we had as many selves as we had interpersonal relations.[3]

In the years since Mitchell introduced the idea of multiplicity into relational psychoanalysis, it has become a central aspect of the theory, and it directly affects our understanding of enactments (see especially Bromberg, 1998a; Davies, 1996; Steven Stern, 2002). In fact, as Benjamin (2010) suggests, our theory of multiplicity is what allows us to recognize the inevitability of enactments. Benjamin writes, "We accept them [enactments] as opportunities to engage experiences that have been and continue to be dissociated, though not necessarily unconscious, but that can be recognized only through dramatization and interaction of parts of our self" (p. 117). It is precisely this connection between multiplicity, enactment, and dramatization that we elaborate throughout this book, culminating in the metaphor of the dance party.

One of Mitchell's most memorable cases is that of Carla (Mitchell, 1997), the daughter of a brilliant, crackpot, paranoid, would-be inventor who came to Mitchell for a second treatment following a first analysis in which she had been a low-fee training case. Mitchell was seeing her once a week at a reduced fee when she discovered that her insurance policy would pay a considerable amount toward her treatment, with a lifetime limit of $20,000. Carla was not sure what she should do. On one hand, she had improved considerably while working with Mitchell and was tempted to see him more frequently; on the other hand, this was a lifetime limit and so she wanted to be absolutely sure that this treatment would work, as it was probably the last chance at an analysis she would ever be able to afford. Mitchell first attempted a form of neutrality on this question, but she increasingly pressured him to give his expert opinion. Mitchell struggled with the meaning of her pressuring him, but he increasingly felt that withholding any of his own thoughts from her was somehow sadistic and self-serving. What were some of Mitchell's thoughts?

> One line of association about the question of whether or not this was the best treatment for her led to the thought: "Beats the hell out of me." Most of the people I've worked with have gotten a great deal out of the work and feel it was worth it, but not all. Would it work for her? I really didn't know. She would have to decide one way or the other and take her chances: "You pays your money and you takes your choice." But that didn't feel right, it felt too facile. Did I really feel so casual about this decision? No. Maybe I should tell her to go ahead and use this money on our analytic work. That was certainly what I would do . . . But that didn't feel very comfortable either. For one thing, I tend to spend money impulsively. The next $20,000 I stumble across will surely pay for the tennis court I've spent years fantasizing about.
>
> (p. 56)

Mitchell described beginning to feel suffocated, a feeling that he came to regard as an inevitable sign that something important was happening.

> This situation is set up so that there is no way for me to be my idea of an analyst. If I abstain, she feels it is an abandonment. If I encourage her, she feels it as a seduction, and there is something in the way our interaction develops that draws me into wanting to make claims and implied promises I have no business making. We seemed to be at an impasse.
>
> (p. 57)

Mitchell wrote that he had not discovered any general solution to situations like these, "But one reaction to impasses that I have found helpful sometimes is an outburst" (p. 57). Mitchell explicitly said that he did not mean a temper tantrum or a retaliatory attack, a point that we especially want to underscore in light of Greenberg's (2001) important critique of the relational literature as fostering the idealization of frame breaking. Mitchell discussed impasses and outbursts, but his notion of outbursts did not refer to impulsiveness or interactional explosiveness. By "outburst," Mitchell meant enacting a dramatic dialogue with the patient, a reaction that conveys that he felt trapped by binary options that both seemed unacceptable to him. It was by finding "the third" that Mitchell enabled therapeutic action and traction. This is precisely how Mitchell felt when pondering many of the polarized options that fill the psychoanalytic literature. It was precisely his refusal to suffocate under the weight of these binary oppositions that led not only to his clinical outbursts but also to his theoretical breakthroughs. With Carla, this insight led to his explaining to her his sense of being stymied:

> I agreed with her that it did not seem fair not to say what I thought, but I could think of only two ways to respond, and neither seemed quite right . . . I told her what I thought I'd be asking myself if I were her: Did she feel the things we were talking about were at the center of what mattered to her in her life? Did she feel we were grappling with them in a way that seemed meaningful? What seemed to her to be a reasonable trial period for our efforts to bear fruit? As I spoke and she engaged some of the questions I was framing, the whole emotional tone between us shifted. I no longer felt that I was dodging her questions, stranded between unacceptable postures. She no longer felt frustrated and subtly abandoned.
>
> (Mitchell, 1997, p. 58)

As mentioned, Mitchell came to recognize his suffocation with patients as a signal that something important was happening in the analysis. When he began to feel trapped, rather than becoming frustrated or simply rebellious, he came to understand that feeling ensnared by a closed world of opposing relational configurations and clashing binary principles "was precisely the sort of trap" in which he needed to be caught (1993, p. 200). His ingenious theoretical innovations, like his creative clinical choices, were the result of learning to identify, tolerate, and sustain these entrapped states, until he could free his imagination and gradually discover some third avenue on which to proceed. Mitchell always valued having options in life, which would maximize his sense of agency, freedom, and choice, and this is a value that he taught to those he loved. It was a value that would ultimately lead him to champion a psychological model of multiplicity and the participation in the clinical situation of his multiple self-states. What Mitchell calls a "clinical outburst" was indeed what Ferenczi had referred to as entering a dramatic dialogue. Rather than interpretation, an explanation of the patient's dynamics from a position outside, independent, objective, or neutral—meaning equidistant from the various agencies of the patient's mind—Mitchell spoke to the patient from within the relationship, enacting the various characters on the analytic stage, thus elaborating them and putting them into dramatic dialogue, overcoming the splits and dissociations that had previously made him feel so trapped and suffocated.

After struggling with himself about how to respond to Carla, Mitchell shared with her the kinds of questions that he would be asking himself if he were her. Did she feel the things they were talking about were at the center of what mattered to her in her life? Did she feel that they were grappling with these issues in a way that seemed meaningful? It is important to see that what Mitchell is presenting to Carla is not the answers to her questions, but he is also not just questioning her. He is showing her, live and in person, the kind of dialogue that he has with himself. He is opening his mind to her and sharing his conflict and his multiplicity. He is modeling this kind of standing in the spaces for her and with her, but it is not a technically planned or calculated decision. Rather, he starts talking with her not knowing exactly where he is going, or what he is going to say, but in the very process of opening himself up the feeling in the room changes, the tone shifts, and that is what he means by an "outburst."

Mitchell may not have consciously planned this as a technical tactic or maneuver, but his expertise as a therapist lay in his unconscious, procedural knowledge of how to sense where a patient is going. Good dancers are not consciously thinking about their steps but are listening to the music and feeling, anticipating, and reacting to their partner's movements. Mitchell's outbursts were not impulsive or destructive; rather, his bursting out of himself, out of his own constraints, was simply taking new steps in the dance (Ringstrom, 2001). Once again, as we have seen before, a dramatic dialogue isn't melodramatic or sensational, but can be subtle, simple, and may involve quiet inactivity. The drama is always there, even when it is unseen, and as we will demonstrate in our next chapter, we always live something together with our patients while we try to get in touch with the truths of the session.

Notes

1 Of course, linking is linked to splitting, and this brings us to Bion only by skipping over Melanie Klein, but see her (1955) paper, "On identification," where she analyses Julian Green's novel *If I Were You* (compare to our "I wish I were you" and its connection to greed and envy) in terms of entering and possessing multiple other selves through projective identification.

2 For a more detailed discussion of Mitchell's theoretical and clinical work, see Aron (2003a).

3 It should be added that Sullivan's personifications are like Jung's complexes in highlighting multiplicity. It is important and relevant to our proposal that Mitchell was strongly influenced by Searles' ideas on multiplicity (see Chapter 6) and especially by the ideas of Bollas and Ogden, both of whom brought post-Bionian thinking to the mix. Thus, we suggest that it is not a matter of adding Bionian ideas to relational psychoanalysis, but rather that relational psychoanalysis was influenced by Bionian formulations, and other British object relations perspectives, from early on in its history, especially by Mitchell, who blended these British influences with his American interpersonal background.

Chapter 5

The truth of the session

Antonino Ferro is, for good reason, one of the most widely read and studied writers in today's psychoanalytic world. Ferro offers a "field theory" approach emphasizing transformation through co-narration, dreaming the session, rather than interpretation. Efforts have begun to compare Ferro's Italian post-Bionian theory with the American interpersonal-relational tradition. This chapter extends this work of comparative psychoanalysis by focusing on the dramatic point of view inherent to both Ferro's narrative and field-theory approach and to the emphasis on enactment in relational and interpersonal theories. Detailed examination of several of Ferro's cases is provided.

Life as a dream

On that morning, when I opened the door to greet Jonathan, he quickly ran into my office and closed the door behind him.

"Did you really do that?" he asked with some worry in his voice.

"Did I really do what?" I responded immediately.

"What do you mean?" Jonathan sounded annoyed. "You double booked. There is another man sitting out there, in your waiting room." He went on, "It's an older man in a suit and tie. Maybe a successful businessman, not a young guy like me, but someone with money, someone with a job, who I bet actually pays for therapy and doesn't rely on his father for that." Jonathan looked at me and said slowly, "The man in your waiting room was waiting for you to open the door, and I made up my mind to not let him win. I knew I was going to run inside and be the first one." He smiled and added, "I guess now you have to ask him to come on another day."

I was pretty fascinated by this description, and even if confused for a moment, I knew, no, I didn't double book. The man in my waiting room wasn't waiting for his appointment with me. But he was certainly a passive participant in Jonathan's active internal drama.

"Now I understand why you quickly ran in," I said, and Jonathan took a deep breath. "Yup," he smiles, "and I won."

"You did," I said. "You did, even if I didn't double book."

Jonathan was silent for a second and looked at me a bit confused. "He isn't waiting for his appointment?" He pointed at the door, said, "So I wonder who that man is?" and then added, "And by the way, I know last time I said I'll bring a dream, but I totally forgot all of them."

I smiled and said, "But I actually think you did bring a dream."

Jonathan looked at me, amused, and I continued, "And in your dream you came to see your therapist. In her waiting room, there is another man. An older man in a suit and tie. Maybe a successful business man, not a young guy like you, but someone with money, someone with a job, someone who probably pays for his own therapy. And you knew that you needed to win. Does that sound right?"

"Yes, I couldn't let him win. I had to fight."

Jonathan and I knew that he brought into the room the exact reality he needed to examine, the drama of his internal life that included three characters: him, a young man in his mid-20s; his father, a business man with money, a suit and a tie; and the room, which represents the entrance into the mother's body but also the exit into the real world. At that point, Jonathan's process included his wish to have a penis as big as his father's, not only as part of the traditional Oedipal narrative of having Mother for himself, but also as representative of having his own power in the world. My waiting room was occupied by the powerful father, since everything in the world belonged to his father, including his therapist and his therapy.

In what we refer to as his dream, the therapist double booked; he and his father were both waiting for the door to open, and in the analysis, the work is to transform the conscious thoughts into unconscious dream material. In some ways, that is one of the differences between the Freudian idea of dream analysis (making the unconscious conscious) and the Bionian idea of transforming conscious to unconscious. Following Bion's ideas on dreams and reverie and authors like Ogden (2007b), who wrote about "talking as dreaming," Ferro offered the technique of using the patient's narratives as dreams. Ferro is well known for having advocated that "we should precede everything the patient says (as well as everything that we say) with the words 'I dreamt that'" (Civitarese & Ferro, 2013, p. 208). The rationale for this suggestion is to avoid literalism and naïve realism, and instead to hear absolutely everything as open and alive to a play of meaning and shifting significance. This approach, referred to as the "oneiric paradigm" (Civitarese, 2005), facilitates the exploration of the waking dream thoughts. It allows patient and analyst to give everything that is said in the analysis the "as if" quality of dreaming. These ideas maintain the essential ambiguity of the psychoanalytic situation in which each thing or event in the field is understood at the same time as something else (a principle articulated by Baranger & Baranger in 1961–1962; see Baranger & Baranger, 2008, p. 799). Both the patient and the analyst keep in mind this "as if" or dreamlike quality of the psychoanalytic situation.

Bionian field theory is a popular approach to contemporary psychoanalytic theory and practice. Field theory has generated excitement and enthusiasm, not only because of its practical usefulness for clinicians, but also because it offers a way of thinking that seems to bridge the divide among various heretofore alternative psychoanalytic schools.

S. Montana Katz (2016) describes the historical, philosophical, and clinical contexts for the development of field theory in South America, North America, and Europe. She views field theory as a family of related bi-personal psychoanalytic perspectives falling into three principal models, which developed relatively independently. The first model is based upon the work of Madeleine and

Willy Baranger and South American psychoanalysis. The second draws upon what is held in common by American interpersonal, intersubjective, relational, and motivational systems' psychoanalytic perspectives, which she describes as implicit field theories. The third is based upon the work of Antonino Ferro and his colleagues in Italy. Katz suggests that in spite of the differences among these three models, they nevertheless offer a new unifying paradigm for psychoanalysis. In many ways we agree, and the model of unconscious dialogue that we suggest in this book is in fact a variety of field theory. But in agreement with Bleger (1969/2012), we believe that the dramatic model has the advantage over the field theory paradigm of emphasizing what is most characteristically human, what Merton Gill (1983) called a "person point of view," rather than a mechanistic metaphor of forces, vectors, and energies.

In an extended panel published in *Psychoanalytic Dialogues* in 2013, as well as in his more recent (2015) book, Donnel Stern set out to systematically compare and contrast the North American version of field theory—interpersonal-relational psychoanalysis (IRP), based on the early work of Harry Stack Sullivan—with Bionian Field Theory (BFT), and this important scholarship led to heated debate and controversy. While we are deeply appreciative of Stern's groundbreaking scholarship, and of the probing arguments of the many commentators, we are going to refrain from a detailed review of this debate. For our purposes, we prefer to dive into clinical material presented by Bionian field theorists so that we stay close to clinical experience. We hope to show that the dramatic approach and the theme of "dramatic dialogue" capture a good deal of the common ground among these theorists and can be clearly seen in clinical presentations.

Although field theory was central to Harry Stack Sullivan's theorizing about interpersonal relations, Stern (2013) points out that it was largely implicitly assumed rather than explicated. Stern further argues that contemporary relational theorists follow Sullivan in this regard, though hardly mentioning field theory as it is taken for granted. In like fashion, Winnicott, Fairbairn, and Kohut theorize with an implicit, even if not fully elaborated or carefully articulated, field theory. For Sullivan, and for these major object relations theorists, as for contemporary relational analysts, all human beings operate within an interpersonal field, and even when alone, one's experience is continuously shaped by the interpersonal fields in which one has been shaped. Thus, in psychotherapy, the therapist cannot avoid co-creating and co-participating in a two-person field. Since one both observes and participates within an interpersonal field, the method of psychotherapy must be participant-observation. In essence, and here we agree with Katz (2016), the shift from a one-person to a two-person psychology that was so central to relational theorizing is indeed another version of field theory.

South American field theory has its origins a generation later than Sullivan, in the work of Madeleine and Willy Baranger in Argentina and Uruguay in the 1960s and 1970s. The Barangers explicitly acknowledge that their field theory relates to a shift from a one-person to a two-person psychology, but much more than Sullivan, they are strongly identified with the psychoanalytic mainstream emphasis on unconscious aspects of the field and of unconscious communication. Like all mainstream analysts, and especially like the Kleinians, they paid special attention to unconscious phantasy. But instead of thinking of phantasy as it exists only in the individual's mind, they drew from Bion's group work to postulate the field as jointly constructed unconscious phantasy that culminates in something more than the sum of its parts. In other words, the field is an emergent property of the jointly constructed phantasies of two people. In this reading of Bion, to which we subscribe, the mind itself is a group composed of dramatis personae, characters or actors, personifications and self-states, as these are described in a variety of theories. The patient–analyst dyad is then a group of two: two complex systems that together generate a field larger than the sum of its parts.

Stern's main point is that there is one fundamental difference between the Barangers' field theory and that of Sullivan and contemporary relational field theorists. The Barangers tend to assume, along with most mainstream and Kleinian analysts, that analysts can generally, under most circumstances, control their countertransference, at least to the extent that it affects their behavior. In that sense, the

Barangers' model emphasizes the bi-personal field, inter-phantasy, or intersubjectivity, whereas relationalists highlight interaction and mutual enactment. Stern explains this difference as based on the traditional psychoanalytic emphasis on phantasy as internal phenomena. While the Barangers in many respects shifted to a fully two-person psychology, nevertheless, for them, phantasy remained at heart an individual unconscious experience. While the Barangers could recognize that the analyst inevitably got caught up in unconscious phantasy, they did not think that this unconscious phantasy would inevitably affect their behavior and thus be enacted in action. In stark contrast, Stern argues that for interpersonal and relational field theorists, the field is both experiential and behavioral, existing in internal reality and expressed in external conduct or action.

While we believe that Stern's generalization does capture a broad difference in emphasis, here we want to demonstrate that projective identification, as Bion originally described it, is not just a phantasy in the individual mind. Nor, in spite of general misconception, does Bion present projective identification as some mysterious mystical process that is constituted only by unconscious phantasy. Quite to the contrary. Read Bion's (1962b) own words in defining projective identification as a normal phenomenon: "As a realistic activity it shows itself as behaviour reasonably calculated to arouse in the mother feelings of which the infant wishes to be rid" (p. 308). Bion repeatedly calls projective identification realistic, rather than rooted in omnipotent phantasy, and he repeatedly emphasizes that it is behavioral, that the infant or patient behaves in such a way to solicit a specific response from the mother or analyst. Bion goes so far as to argue that the infant has a rudimentary sense of reality and therefore can observe the other realistically enough to learn how to behaviorally elicit certain responses from her. To us, it seems crystal clear that whatever else the term *projective identification* may evoke, for Bion, it is a realistic, behavioral, interpersonal, two-person concept. This is hardly limited to phantasy, as Stern would have it in his description of post-Bionians. However, Stern may nevertheless be correct in his depiction of some post-Bionians, as each so-called post-Bionian theorist takes what they like from Bion, reads Bion in their own way, and develops some concepts and not others. Hence, as we turn to Ferro, among the most prominent of post-Bionians, we need to consider which aspects of Bion he utilizes in producing his dreamy filmic version of Bion, and which pieces end up on the cutting-room floor.

Antonino Ferro and Giuseppe Civitarese are among the most prolific authors within the post-Bionian psychoanalytic tradition. Influenced and supervised by mainstream London Kleinians, Ferro reacted against the narrow technical emphasis on explicit, or what he refers to as "saturated," interpretation. Ferro and Civitarese blend Bion's contributions, particularly his ideas about waking dream thoughts (Bion, 1962a), with the Barangers' conceptualiza-tion of field theory, which leads to the idea that patient and analyst are always dreaming the session together. Through joint dreaming, psychoanalysis allows for the development of the mental tools, alpha-betization, that facilitate the development and creation of thought. In this model, the psychoanalytic process is not so much concerned with interpretation—meaning explication, explanation from the outside, "decoding"—but instead, according to Ferro (2006), inter-pretation extends to "a mythic narration" (p. 990). This means that the patient's associations, their material and communications, are transposed into "a script, narrative, or filmic form, which actualizes and renders visible what is being said" (p. 991). In Chapter 7, we will build on these ideas of Ferro in discussing Ogden's work on psychoanalysis as dreaming.

Ferro says that the classical understanding of interpretation is often replaced "by the activities of the analyst, which activate transforma-tions in the field, transformations which can also derive from the changing of the analyst's mental state, from minimal interventions that function as enzymes" (p. 991). What is it exactly that Ferro is suggesting to replace the more traditional decoding interpretations or saturated interpretations, explanations provided from outside of the patient's mind, and directed toward the one-person psychology of the patient? Ferro is advocating that the analyst is part of the field and that any change in the analyst, even a change in attitude or alertness, leads to changes in the field as a whole. But what is the analyst trying to do?

What does Ferro mean by transposing the patient's material into narrative, script, or filmic versions? A significant hint is provided by Ferro when he says that his method is related to that of Ekstein and Wallerstein's ideas (1956) about "interpreting within the metaphor" (Ferro, 2006, p. 1001). The Ekstein and Wallerstein paper is a classic of psychoanalytic child play therapy. In contradistinction to Klein's interpretative technique, Ekstein and Wallerstein argued that it was often much wiser for the analyst to stay within the patient's metaphors rather than interpreting them from the outside, which they believed would more than likely disrupt the child's play elaborations (which is of course similar to drama therapy; see Emuna, 1994; Jennings, 1997; Landy, 1986, 1993). More recently, Ferro and Civitarese (2015) explain that what is at times so difficult to grasp about the clinical application of field theory appears rather obvious when viewed through the lens of child analysis where everything is play.

Ferro correctly links this idea to Winnicott's clinical approach with its emphasis on the development of transitional play space. For Winnicott, psychoanalysis is modeled on a squiggle game where patient and analyst each contribute to the play, neither remaining outside of the play space. As Winnicott (1971) notes, "psychotherapy has to do with two people playing together" (p. 38).

In explicating his and Ferro's model, Civitarese (2005, 2013) elaborates the longstanding analytic metaphor (originating in Freud, as we saw in Chapter 3) of the theater and the co-production of plays and films as the core metaphor for analytic work. His account of character, auditioning actors, casting, and choosing the appropriate genre enriches the model. In theater, as in analysis, disbelief is suspended, drama highlights the "as if" potential space, in which characters, objects, and narratives represent our internal dramas (Farber, 2014).

Let's stay with the question of precisely what it is that Ferro is advocating regarding the technique of adult analysis. Ferro is clearly and deliberately drawing on his experience as a child therapist steeped in play. With adults, he is suggesting that psychoanalysis is a highly verbal and dialogic form of creative arts therapy, a play therapy for adults. The analyst is not there to comment on the play from the audience's perspective but rather is there to join in the play and to help develop it further from the inside. (Later, we will utilize Ogden's similar idea of becoming at one with the patient's unconscious reality.) Scripts, narrations, or filmic versions are all forms of aesthetic modulation, transformations of the patient's material into artistic productions. Very much like Jung before him, Joyce McDougall and Zvi Lothane as we extrapolate and extend them in Chapter 3, and in line with his colleagues James Grotstein and Thomas Ogden, Ferro and Civitarese are suggesting a form of psychoanalytic creative dialogue, a verbal squiggle game. The patient's internal objects or self-states are depicted as "characters" who need to be brought onto the analytic stage where they are elaborated and developed. Each exchange between patient and analyst may be thought of as a "scene," and in each scene that is staged the character may be further developed and symbolized, or "cooked," which means transformed, further processed, and developed.

In this model, it is not only the patient's internal world that provides the characters. The point of field theory is that a group situation is activated between patient and analyst so the dramatis personae, whether brought to the analytic stage by patient or analyst, are not regarded as real characters or only internal objects, but are thought to be "holograms" that represent the functioning of the field (Ferro & Civitarese, 2015, p. 111). The field transforms everything brought by patient and analyst into characters that are used to "navigate" the analytic journey.

Ferro's descriptions and language have become increasingly and more strikingly like our usage of dramatic dialogue. Ferro now refers directly to "transformation in drama" (Ferro & Nicoli, 2017, p. 136) and links together transformation in drama with transformation in dream, in game, and in narrative. Ferro also argues that we are not just playing with, dramatizing, or dreaming the patient's material but that it is evident that analysts also introduce their own metaphors and characters onto the analytic stage, co-constructing a mutually transformative scene. We can see the dramatic emphasis of Ferro's approach in his enthusiasm for the analyst who is foremost a magician: "The analyst transforms internal reality, exorcises demons, rides dragons: he opens up a space for imagination, creativity, the absurd, and the unthought" (Ferro & Nicoli, 2017, p. 6). Consider this illustration of Ferro's approach of transformation in drama:

> If the patient is hypochondriac and has a liver problem, I have to take a spaceship and fly with him to where his liver is. Our movie opens with two young aliens landing on a large reddish mass, which is this planet called liver. There we have to go, so begins the movie, *The Red Planet.*
>
> (Ferro & Nicoli, 2017, p. 129)

Here is one short vignette presented by Ferro that we use here to clarify what we mean and what we understand Ferro is implying when we refer to putting each character on stage.

Guido is a psychiatrist who works in an Italian prison where most of the inmates are Arab immigrants. Early in his analysis, he tells Ferro about his work with these Arabs. Ferro considers the obvious interpretations of this narrative; for example, he might interpret to Guido that he is afraid to come into contact in the analysis with undiscovered, foreign, dangerous aspects of himself. In addition, Ferro might interpret to Guido that he was also afraid that Ferro was a threatening stranger who would be incomprehensible to him, speaking a foreign tongue. Ferro, illustrating his technical warning against explicit or saturated interpretation, emphasizes that he makes neither of these interpretations. But he does not refrain from interpreting out of fear that the interpretations are premature, as perhaps an ego psychologist might, out of considerations of timing and layering of defenses, but rather because he has a different goal in mind. His goal, following Bion, is not to make the unconscious conscious, that is, he does not want to decode who these Arabs are symbolically in Guido's unconscious inner world. Rather, he wants to encourage Guido to develop a discourse on these Arabs so that each and every individual Arab prisoner would become increasingly recognizable, differentiated, and remarkable for his own characteristics. Each Arab prisoner is invited onto the analytic stage where they may become increasingly differentiated, developed, and may then be experientially engaged in the dream field.

Ferro assumes that each reference to an individual prisoner in Guido's narrative is a carrier for a nuance of emotion. Ferro is not in a rush to decode or make explicit what things mean. Rather than making the unconscious conscious, he is helping to take what Guido thinks is conscious and make it unconscious, that is, to get away from the real and literal and help Guido dream. Using his oneiric paradigm, when Guido says, "I was at the prison yesterday and an Arab prisoner frightened me," Ferro hears this as if Guido said, "Yesterday I had a dream that I was in a prison and an Arab prisoner frightened me." This oneiric method is meant to encourage Guido to keep meanings loose and in flux. By elaborating each character, Ferro encourages the underlying emotions to be further focalized, modulated, and metabolized while always staying within Guido's metaphor, not disrupting the narrative, but encouraging each character to come on stage and play out their unique scenes, thus transforming the narrative through dramatic dialogue.

As we have seen, Stern suggested that the difference between the interpersonal and relational field theorists and the post-Bionian field theorists has to do with the recognition that the analyst's behavior, action, or conduct is implicated, not just their fantasies. We have shown that Bion himself clearly emphasized that projective identification involved behavior and conduct as well as phantasy. Ferro realizes and even emphasized that his conduct matters. He even goes so far as to acknowledge that the analyst's subtlest shifts in attitude and states of alertness influence the field and contribute to the elaboration of the patient's characters. Nevertheless, we do continue to see a difference in emphasis between Ferro and Civitarese in contrast to the relational writers. For Ferro, the majority of projective identifications go from the patient to the analyst. While he acknowledges that sometimes the analyst may project into the patient, he writes as an example, "In this case, a tired, defended, unavailable or suffering analyst can evacuate his anxiety into the patient's mind" (2006, p. 990). The relational analyst in us is tempted to interrupt here and say to Ferro, "Really, is there any other kind of analyst?" In other words, what for Ferro remains an atypical or unusual event is for the relationalist something much more continuous, as the analyst is caught up in ongoing enactments along with the patient. Or to return to Stern's (2013) point, the relational therapist is much more likely to view the analyst's unconscious as expressed in conduct that regularly and continuously affects the field. Again, as we have suggested, each post-Bionian takes what they select from among Bion's many contributions and interprets Bion idiosyncratically. There is no single right way to read or use him. By focusing on Bion's "waking dream thoughts," it may be that Ferro leans more toward phantasy and play and may be relatively less focused on behavior and conduct. Furthermore, since his goal is to enter a dream state with his patients, to get too focused on the meanings of his own behavior and conduct might interrupt his process and wake him up from the dreamy state of consciousness that he is trying to create and develop. In other words, the self-reflection (consciously examining their own participation) that interpersonalists and relationalists so often rely on as central features of their methodology might at the same time interfere with the creation of a mutual dream state. In more classical terms, this might have been stated in the language of facilitating an adaptive regression, a regression in the service of the ego, in both patient and analyst (Aron & Bushra, 1998).

Good and bad objects/new and old objects

In what immediately became a classic of the relational literature, Jay Greenberg (1986) suggested that neutrality be defined not in terms of behavior but in terms of the goals of the analysis. He argued that we keep the term *neutrality* not to mean indifference or lack of participation on the part of the analyst, but rather, "Neutrality embodies the goal of establishing an optimal tension between the patient's tendency to see the analyst as an old object and his capacity to experience him as a new one" (p. 97). What Greenberg means by this is that some behaviors on the analyst's part lend themselves to his or her being viewed by the patient as an old object, similar to the patient's significant objects, usually the parents, and other behaviors lend themselves to the analyst being seen as new or different from the parents. For example, if a patient describes his father as uptight and withholding, then an analyst behaving with abstinence, reluctant to provide gratification, may contribute to the analyst's being viewed as like the patient's father, whereas that analyst's looseness and generosity will likely emphasize that the analyst is a new object. Here, Greenberg focuses on the split between the perception of the analyst as the old/bad object and the good/new object. He suggests that neutrality implies that the analyst overcomes this splitting by maintaining the tension between these two positions, rather than collapsing into one or the other. He writes, "If the analyst cannot be experienced as a new object, analysis never gets under way; if he cannot be experienced as an old one, it never ends" (p. 98).

Since Greenberg's article appeared, this idea of maintaining tension between these approaches has been highlighted in the relational and self-psychological literature. Steven Stern (1994) has argued for an integration of "needed relationships" and "repeated relationships." Stern suggests that patients actively seek to enlist the therapist both in old pathogenic interactional scenarios and in new therapeutically needed relational configurations. As the self-psychologist Anna Ornstein (1974) suggests, the patient's curative fantasy encompasses both the past and the future in the sense that it is not only a repetition of the past but also an expression of hope for a new and different future. For Ornstein, it is hope that primarily "fuels" the patient's commitment in the therapeutic relationship. The emphasis, therefore, on patients' "need to repeat" the past in their therapeutic relationships must be shifted to include the "dread to repeat." As we point out in our chapters on the prospective function and generative enactment, this is closely related to the self-psychological emphasis on the leading edge over the trailing edge of interpretation.

It is not only that some patients, at certain moments, need more of a new object or an old object, or a good or bad object, or a needed or repeated relationship, or a leading-edge versus trailing-edge interpretation. It is also the case that various schools of analysis emphasize one side of this tension more than the other. As an obvious example, we believe that the classical school tends to emphasize the repeated relationship, whereas self psychology tends toward the needed relationship, what was traditionally considered a "corrective emotional experience." Furthermore, analysts vary along these lines because of their own personality characteristics, or because of who they have become at a particular moment with a particular patient. In Chapter 7, we will comment further on the ambiguity of being an old and new object.

Analyzing Ferro and Civitarese's work, we find that they lean toward being new objects, different from the primal objects. They are more likely to respond within their dramatic dialogue in such a way that the patient is encouraged to view them as new and different from the parents. Consider Ferro analyzing a patient who says that as a child his father never took him by the hand but just expected him to perform well at school and hired tutors to ensure his success, and rather than providing support the father would sometimes beat him. The first question that Ferro asks himself is how he would intervene so as to bring about a transformation that would allow his patient to stop perceiving him as an unfeeling father who sternly considers his academic performance. Ferro goes on to ask how he might modify his interpretive style, his approach, or even his mental state to encourage such a transformation. Here, we see how his clinical approach leans toward interpreting in a way that elicits his being seen as a new good object, rather than the old traumatizing object.

Some might pause here and question, why should the analyst do anything to interfere with how the patient views her? Why does the analyst have a preference to be viewed as different from the traumatizing father? In fact, some analysts might suggest that this attitude constitutes a refusal to accept the negative transference, that it is a transference manipulation or the rejection of a projection. What is the real objection to this stance? Some would suggest (such as more classical analysts; see for example Lasky, 1993) that what the patient most needs is precisely the experience of reliving their early developmental trauma so that they could now, as an adult, rework that trauma and better integrate it in their minds. To the degree that the analyst refuses to play the role of the bad old object, the traumatizing object, they deprive the patient of what they most need.

In short, according to this critique, and as we describe later, this was precisely Searles' critique of many analysts. Searles consistently maintained the opposite clinical assumption, entertaining a much darker perspective, namely that the analyst must embody the negative transference so that the patient could relive their developmental trauma within the analysis in vivo.

Luca and the wine cellar

Ferro (2006) introduces Luca by telling us that for a long time he was not able to tolerate any closeness in the transference, and Ferro focuses on a critical moment when he believed that Luca had become more receptive to his interpretations. Luca's distance was so intense that he did not refer to his analyst by name but spoke in the third person about "Luca and his analyst." Ferro indicates that he oscillated between a decoding interpretive register, along the lines of traditional interpretation, and a containing transformative register, intervening by staying within the manifest communication, not disrupting the narrative.

When the Christmas break arrived, Luca told Ferro that he had bought a special saucepan that was able to cook polenta automatically, without anyone manually stirring it. His next association was of his wish to buy a walkie-talkie that could communicate across great distances. Next, he associated to buying four cases of oranges that would last him through the Christmas separation.

Ferro then intervenes by telling Luca that "the days seemed long gone when during separations he would need to plug in his Duracell batteries which would assure him complete autonomy, whereas now he could equip himself for the holiday, making use of a series of instruments which allow us to stay in contact" (p. 1000). Luca's first reaction was seemingly to accept this interpretation, but he immediately associated to his mother-in-law (always a bad sign? Is the mother-in-law the new archetype that, like the stepmother in fairytales, holds the split-off negative characteristics of the mother?). Luca detests his mother-in-law, who once entered his wine cellar and uncorked some bottles without asking his permission. Ferro infers that Luca is communicating to him, through this narrative derivative, that he was not yet ready to hear the interpretation Ferro had given him. Luca went on to say that his mother-in-law talked to him relentlessly, so much so that she neglected her grandchildren, who then missed their mother and cried endlessly.

Ferro chose not to make an explicit transference interpretation along the lines that the analyst was the mother-in-law who uncorked meanings before Luca was ready, and who talked too much, interpreted too much, and neglected the child part of Luca, who just wanted his mother's presence. By waiting and not making this interpretation, Ferro believes that he facilitated the analytic process such that Luca could go on to his next association, which was of his mother, who called him with an affectionate and well-timed phone call.

We want to make a few points about this beautiful case illustration and want to be clear that we are deeply appreciative of Ferro's clinical expertise. Our comments are made in a spirit of fostering a dialogue between his approach and a more interpersonal-relational approach, not to disparage one or the other, but to contribute to an appreciation of what each has to offer the other. We certainly feel that we have learned from both schools of thought and practice.

When reading this case, we miss Ferro's self-reflections, specifically about his own contribution to Luca's developing relationship with him. This perhaps seems to contradict that the very purpose of Ferro's example is to show how he is considering and reflecting on his premature interpretation and Luca's reaction to it. Ferro, in spite of Donnel Stern's (2013) generalizations, certainly is interested in his own behavior or conduct. He recognizes that his interpretation is an activity that impacts the patient, and that the patient's next associations comment on the analyst's behavior. Nevertheless, Ferro does not ask, or alert the reader to wonder, what it was that he was feeling, or who it was that he had become at that moment, such that he felt the need to address his relationship with Luca so directly. He attributes this entirely to his recognition that Luca seemed more ready to hear it, and in doing so neglects anything at all about his own felt need to address Luca directly. Notice that he tells Luca, who had until then referred to his analyst and himself in the third person, that these instruments allow "us" to stay in contact. It is Ferro, in this illustration, who introduces that there is an "us." As far as we know, Luca had never spoken of an "us." At no point in his written presentation does Ferro wonder whether there was anything about himself—his personal style, his feelings about Luca, his analytic approach, anything—that might have contributed to Luca's distance, and at no point does he ask himself why he now felt a need to address their closeness and distance directly—not because of his understanding of what the patient might have needed or been ready to hear, but because of Ferro's own personal needs. This is an especially relevant question, since the vignette appears in an article that downplays these explicit interpretations and warns of their dangers, and therefore we wonder why Ferro would not pay more attention to, or maybe doesn't share with the reader, his own subjective experience at those moments when he in fact makes these explicit interpretations.

In addition, while Ferro's approach is carefully designed to listen to the patient's feedback about each and every intervention, nevertheless, Ferro continues to adopt a position of "knowing" that retains a certain degree of unacknowledged authoritarianism. All of us, from all schools of thought, may respond at times with authoritarian styles, but what we are examining here is an aspect of authoritarianism that is not personal, but rather implicit in the theoretical approach itself. What we mean is that Ferro is very open to hearing his patient's unconscious communication of feedback about the impact of his interpretation as premature, and is open, attentive, responsive, and seeking correction. Nevertheless, he then hears his patient's response (for example, the description of his detested mother-in-law), and he concludes its significance on his own, unilaterally. While he listens to the patient's next association, and from that point of view he remains open, there is an endless loop where with each turn *he* decides what the patient's response must mean.

Here is another example: When the patient associates to his affectionate mother, Ferro infers that this feedback indicates that his own non-interpretive waiting was experienced as her "well-timed phone call." One might question whether Ferro has the tendency to listen for indications that he is the good mother, the new object, and to move away too quickly from owning his own mother-in-law self. The patient may unconsciously know that and have shifted to talking about the good mother as a way of reassuring Ferro that he is not the bad object. Remember that it is not the "real" person Ferro that we are discussing, but rather the "character" Ferro that is the star of his narrative. We wonder about the degree to which we all so wish to be good objects (and/or maybe are afraid of being bad objects) that we convince ourselves that if we are sufficiently attuned to the patient's response, then we will inevitably be experienced as new good objects. We will expand on this notion in Chapter 7.

Another approach might be for the analyst to tell the patient that he found himself wondering if he was talking too much like the mother-in-law. We imagine Ferro would argue that being so explicit in regard to the transference just contributes to the problem, enacting the same dynamic yet again. He suggests that this is the problem with too radical a "relational" approach. But it is also possible that such an intervention, if done with less certainty, and perhaps even with some increased personal involvement, might contribute to breaking this vicious cycle. For example, we could imagine saying to the patient something along the lines of, "Oh, I just referred to 'us' as 'us.' I know we haven't talked about 'us' until now. I wonder if I was also feeling something about the upcoming vacation and was feeling isolated from you, and so I may have felt the need to speak of 'us' as 'us.' Does that make any sense to you?"

This may seem outside of the range of standard technique, and perhaps it might not fit Ferro's style or Luca's. We are not arguing in favor of this intervention, especially if it came out of the blue, in an analysis where the analyst had not spoken that way previously. If an analyst has not spoken that way, however, then isn't it possible that the patient's distance is from the beginning at least partially a reaction to the analyst's style and approach? Our point is not to suggest a better technique or a superior intervention; rather, we introduce this imaginary intercession only to expand possibilities and facilitate points of comparison and contrast.

It might seem as though such an intervention appeals to the patient's conscious response, that their reaction to such a question or self-disclosure is taken as collaborative and therefore accepted at face value. Of course, such an approach would initially disregard the unconscious. An analyst, however, may not ask such questions simply to hear an answer that is taken at face value. Instead, the question is meant to stir up further associations, and the analyst listens to the patient's response attending to both the surface reply, as well as to the way in which the question stirs up unconscious derivative material. Such an attitude maintains a dialectic tension between the hermeneutics of suspicion and the hermeneutics of trust/faith/the sacred (Ricoeur, 1970). It invites the patient's conscious and unconscious collaboration and so provides some check on the analyst's interpretive authority.

Power struggles and homosexual anxiety

In the next case that we will discuss, we want to extend and deepen our pursuit of the point made by Stern (2013), concerning whether post-Bionian field theorists recognize that their own unconscious phantasies, or the joint phantasies of the bi-personal field, are inevitably enacted, actualized in behavior and conduct between the patient and the analyst, with the analyst as co-participant. This, remember, is the central divide between the two schools of thought, according to Stern. We will utilize a clinical example from Civitarese and Ferro (2013) to show that even when analysts are convinced that they are interpreting or just listening, inevitably they are also enacting the interpersonal dynamics of the dyad. In other words, neutrality in its classical sense is not a possibility; one always interacts and co-participates in the mutual dynamics of the field (Levenson, 1972). Furthermore, as we demonstrated earlier, not only do we view enactments as inevitable, but we also suggest that they are often beneficial, essential, and generative.

A simple example concerns Lucio, who begins a session by asserting with some emphasis that he has not had any dreams. He then goes on to say that he had brought his cat into the veterinarian to be neutered. The analyst suggests to the patient that he look at his communication as a dream, and the analyst goes on to interpret Lucio's fear that the analyst's upcoming vacation has fueled his aggression and he feels he must inhibit his aggression and defang or neuter himself.

This brilliant clinical intervention demonstrates the creative technique Civitarese and Ferro are proposing, where the analyst approaches everything the patient says as a dream. It encourages the development of creativity and imagination, playfulness, trust in one's unconscious to communicate and inform, and less reliance on rationality and conventional, linear thinking. Nevertheless, here the analyst's insistence on treating the patient's association as a dream might also be taken as an enactment, an interpersonal ploy, a power move, in which the analyst can override the patient, especially because so much of the content of the vignette seems to revolve around interpersonal dynamics of power and control. We might assume that as part of the enactment this patient emphasized that he had no dreams. One way of looking at this exchange is to think that the patient refused to give something to the analyst, and the analyst that would not take "no" for an answer overrode the patient's answer, insisting that the patient had indeed presented a dream despite his protests to the contrary. Interestingly, the rest of the case leads to discussions of various interpersonal maneuvers, in which one person lubricates their relationship with another. It's important to note here that we don't think such enactments can be avoided by a different or better technique; rather, the analyst inevitably co-participates in the interpersonal dynamics of the dyad.

Compare this case with that of Jonathan, with which we opened this chapter. Here, the analyst is clearly following Ferro's oneiric method of treating everything the patient says as if it began with

"I had a dream that . . ." The analyst playfully invites the patient to dream up the session with her. It is in some ways remarkably close to Ferro's case of Lucio. In both cases, the patients claim that they did not bring any dreams. It seems to us that there is an important difference in that Lucio's assertion occurred in the context of power dynamics. He challenged the analyst who was interested in dreaming, and so in his participation in the enactment Ferro overrode Lucio's challenge by saying, "I treat everything as a dream," with the possible implication that "you cannot resist me by not bringing in a dream." In contrast, in the vignette of Jonathan, it seems to us that his remark was not issued in the same challenging tone, but rather it emerged as a guilty confession, as part of an enactment of an Oedipal drama, in which his analyst participates by saying he won and making him the Oedipal victor. Thus, both cases depict enactments of various kinds.

We end this discussion with a last clinical moment. Here, Ferro (2006) tells us the story of his work with Stefano, who is several years into an analysis. Ferro tells us that, "every excessive interpretive approach can sometimes provoke homosexual anxiety" (p. 1001), but we immediately note that Ferro does not say in whom. Nor does he elaborate on what this means or how he understands this pattern. But he does go on parenthetically to elaborate thoughts about the container–contained, including Bion's famous symbols with their phallic and vaginal connotations, which we infer likely conveys his associating the homosexual panic to penetration and to the genitals.

After several productive analytic sessions, the analyst is expecting Stefano to arrive at his office, but while waiting for him, after the bell rings, he has an intense auditory and visual reverie in which he was quite sure that it was a woman with clacking high-heeled shoes who was climbing the stairs to his office. Ferro acknowledges that this experience shook him up, that he was puzzled and perplexed and tried to eliminate his thought, but felt an urgency to interpret this disturbing experience. Finally, Ferro settles on an explanation that we believe serves to regulate him. He concludes that his reverie was his way of letting himself know that Stefano has achieved a new receptive capacity. Ferro responds by making a number of transference interpretations and then warns Stefano, in what seems to be a humorous and ironic comment, not to come in the next day and complain that his son has an allergic reaction, which was one way Stefano had previously responded to explicit interpretations. The patient laughs and tells Ferro that he should not pre-empt his moves. Sure enough, in the next session, Stefano has several associations that confirm his sensitivity to penetrating interpretations, such as that his wife was worried that his son swallowed a pin, and of a doctor who increased the patient's dosage without considering side effects. Ferro very dramatically ends this important paper by saying that he decided to not interpret these reactions, but to just adjust his distance and timing.

In this case, the analyst has a dramatic response, his own reaction triggered by a phantasy that his male patient, at least in his associations, has trans-morphed into a woman. He hears a woman's high-heeled shoes clacking on steps, but why would this phantasy make him so anxious? What does it evoke in him? He is quite agitated, but his clinical approach does not encourage him to reflect on what he himself brings to this situation (the analyst's psychology and dynamics). Instead, it points him to look further at the patient. He concludes that through projective identification, his reveries are now capturing what he has concluded about his patient's receptivity. The analyst remains certain that this is about the patient and not about himself. Ferro acknowledges that in response to this recognition, he launches a series of penetrating interpretations, but no thought is given in this paper to the possibility that he, the analyst, had some feelings about penetrating and being penetrated, and that what calms him down is to be the penetrator and not the penetrated, even while thinking of himself as a container. When he shifts quickly from talking about homosexual anxiety in a man to the image of the man now being a woman, this linkage implies a binary in which men are penetrators and women penetrated. We suspect that what regulates him may be that he is back in the position of the phallic penetrator.

Here again, we are not objecting to the analytic couple being caught up in an enactment; rather, we are suggesting that analysts can never only be analytic instruments—neutral observers or interpretive penetrators—but rather are always already participating in dramatic dialogues, where in this case the analyst penetrates, is being penetrated, and reacts to those acts with pleasure, anxiety, and so on.

While Ferro's clinical work looks quite different from that of Harold Searles', to which we turn in the next chapter, and both are quite different from those who practice in a more standard relational way, we highlight their work because of their dramatic presentations, which are deeply engaged and highly influential. Their approaches lend themselves to intense examination and study, and both, while using themselves remarkably differently (each in accordance with their own idiom and character), nevertheless understand what is happening between them and their patients as an ongoing dramatization of centrally important dynamics. Furthermore, each believes that the actual dramatization itself, in the form of dreaming, play, and theater, even more than the interpretation of the dramatization, is transformative and generative.

Chapter 6

Theatrical engagement

Harold Searles pioneered the clinical usefulness of countertransference and was an enormous influence on psychoanalytic work with highly disturbed and disturbing patients. Searles was most proud of his live and videotaped clinical interviews of patients and argued for this method as optimal for teaching psychotherapy. His clinical work is vivid, controversial, and intensely dramatic, even if provocative. Ogden has argued that Searles' clinical approach, while developed independently, closely parallels Bion's theory. This chapter examines his clinical approach, highlighting his advocacy of the analyst dramatizing (authentically) the bad or traumatic object.

Forty years after her long hospitalization as a suicidal teenager, and now a successful mental health professional, Anita Sawyer examined her medical records and reflected on her experiences in psychotherapy through the course of her life. She reviews her years of inpatient treatment but also describes a dramatic interview with Harold Searles, who was at that time her psychiatrist's supervisor.

Sawyer had two such interviews in late 1964. In the first, she dismissed Searles as an "uncomprehending jerk" because he focused on her attempt to be a saint. However, there was a second interview, she says (in her YouTube video—see Sawyer, 2013), "and that one I have always remembered and credited and I knew this even at the time, somehow, with changing my life." "The way Dr. Searles spoke to me in that interview had consequences for the rest of my life" (Sawyer, 2011, p. 780).

In the second interview, Searles again referred to Sawyer as a saint and told her that she looked at him as if she were a frightened young fawn:

> My frozen innocence and fear made him feel like a dirty old man, and this made him feel so bad about himself that he thought of suicide. A remarkable feature of this exchange was that unconsciously I had communicated, and he had received, the essence of a truth I would only discover decades later: my paralyzing fear was indeed connected with a dirty old man. This fact underlay my guilt and consequent obsession with suicide.
>
> (Sawyer, 2011, p. 780)

She importantly adds:

> A transcript of that interaction might appear bizarre or quite inappropriate, however for me, although I couldn't explain it consciously, Dr. Searles made contact. I felt connected and understood. The life-changing aspect was that I could affect the feelings of someone else, especially in this case, a respected authority. I had caused him to feel something. For someone who felt as if she floated alone in the universe, unreal and completely without influence, this was a new concept.
>
> That evening, I told patients gathered at our informal coffee discussion group what had happened in the interview.
>
> "He said that I made him feel guilty, like he was a dirty old man. That I was trying to be some kind of saint. Can you imagine?"
>
> "Hell, yes," said one, "You're always doing stuff for other people."
>
> One after another, my friends and even patients I hardly knew gave examples of my oppressive helpfulness. I felt bewildered. Then I got it. Instead of reacting with guilt and shame, which was my usual response, I felt exhilarated. Dr. Searles had jolted me out of my ordinary frame of reference. From his reaction and then my friends', I grasped the idea that my behavior affected other people: I influenced how they saw themselves, not just what they thought about me.
>
> (Sawyer, 2011, p. 780)

Sawyer's testimony regarding her interview with Harold Searles in 1964 is of historic importance for American psychoanalysis and psychiatry. Several themes are highlighted that help us understand Searles' clinical methodology and his unique ability to engage with patients, often with psychotic patients, with whom none of the hospital staff had been able to make contact. Indeed, this was Searles' reputation: He would routinely make the rounds of psychiatric facilities around the country and interview patients live in front of audiences of psychiatrists and staff. Whatever people thought about his interviews—and indeed people had strong and mixed reactions—there was a solid consensus, among those who saw him live, that he managed to engage patients who were otherwise unreachable.

Sawyer, remembering the interview some 50 years later, describes the interview as life-changing—and remembers that even at the time she knew she had been changed.[1] Searles made deep contact with her by somehow recognizing the underlying themes of suicide, sexual abuse, defensive and manic helpfulness, and underlying grandiosity. Remember that in 1964 sexual abuse and trauma were not being discussed very actively by psychoanalysts, who placed their emphasis on internal, intrapsychic conflict and downplayed external social realities. It would take many more years before trauma and sexual abuse were taken up by the psychiatric and analytic community.

And yet Sawyer also recognizes and warns us that someone looking at the interview from the outside might well consider it both bizarre and inappropriate. Indeed, very often, many in Searles' audience did find him to be bizarre, sometimes psychotic, and inappropriately offensive and aggressive or sadistic. Yet here, Sawyer convincingly testifies to the emotional contact made with her.

Of course, we might wonder if the fact that she was an abused child may have contributed to her feeling connected when he was aggressive and sadistic and that her response was masochistic. Sawyer explains both why and how she felt understood in that the analyst touched something about her sexual abuse, guilt, and grandiosity, and she also documents how this helped her communicate with and engage those in the group surrounding her, both at the time and throughout decades afterward. She expresses clearly that by sharing his intense, even suicidal reaction to her, she felt for the first time that she had an impact on an important and powerful person, that she could make him feel. And by communicating this back to her in a way that she could tolerate and process, he completed a cycle of emotional linking where her feelings were unconsciously transferred to him, he processed those feelings, and he returned them to her in a somewhat modified form. This is a perfect illustration of Bion's (1962b) notion of communicative projective identification, containment, and re-projection, such that the patient could gradually learn to metabolize the material—that is, learn to Think.

As we will see in the next illustration of Searles' interviews, it is not accidental that he so quickly picked up on and verbalized thoughts about suicide—that is, life and death. Searles continually maintained an awareness of the emotional and experiential power of life and death forces in patients/people as well as in himself. He used his sensitivity to the theme of life and death to keep his finger directly on the pulse of patients' anxieties.

Splitting

Before moving onto the next illustration, keep in mind how Searles subtly but clearly highlighted the role of splitting. Indeed, as we will demonstrate here, Searles' work was always about the importance of splitting, which he interpreted but also lived or acted out with both patients and colleagues. In Sawyer's case, this is dramatized by the split between his depiction of Sawyer as a saint and himself as a dirty old man, a theme that echoed and also reversed her experience of being powerless, surrounded by powerful psychiatrists, herself being a psychotic, powerless patient, interacting with powerful and fully adult doctors. In sum, while blending a variety of theoretical influences, Searles' approach certainly makes use of and reverberates with the Kleinian/Bionian themes of splitting and projective identification, but always understood as actually being played out in the interaction between patient and therapist or person and family, as he had learned from Sullivan and the Washington, DC interpersonalists. In this regard, Searles was an early relationalist, a precursor of the relational approach in that he blended American interpersonalism with Kleinian object relations and more classical theories. We read him as the prequel to the relational narrative (see Chapter 7). But we will return to theory after examining the second illustration.

Interview from 1993 at the National Institute for the Psychotherapies (NIP)[2]

The following interview was conducted and videotaped at a conference in 1993. It is accompanied by an additional video of Harold Searles explaining to the faculty what he hopes to achieve in doing this kind of interview and expressing his own reactions to watching the video two weeks later. He says that this interview is typical of those he has conducted on a regular basis. He also says that as he watches it, he believes he has the same reactions watching the video that he had during the interview. The only thing that Searles knew in advance is that this patient is in her 20s, an outpatient in psychotherapy, and an actress. He was given her first name on a piece of paper and told not to look at it until after the interview. He tells us that this frustrated him, since he took it as a neurotic controlling manipulation. The following is the first three minutes of the interview:

Harold   We have an hour for our interview and let me suggest to
Searles   you that you let me hear as fully as you can tell me whatever
(HS):   you find yourself experiencing throughout the interview
except insofar as I am interrupting you.

Patient   Okay. Ah . . . Well right now what I am experiencing is a
(P):   slight bit of panic. I'm nervous. My heart is beating. My
hands arc a little clammy. My voice is a little hoarse.

HS: Your heart is beating. That's . . .

P: Faster than usual.

HS: Well, but your heart is beating, you say. That's some evidence that you are alive.

P: Right. [*Chuckles*]

HS: Have you any doubt of that? Do you ever find yourself doubting that, I wonder?

P: No [*shakes head, slight laugh*], I don't doubt that. [*Laughs*]

HS: You don't doubt that. [*Head down, looks dejected*]

P: And, um, otherwise I feel better than I expected to. I thought I would get very nervous about doing this. But I feel okay.

HS: Relief, some relief?

P: To some extent, yeah.

HS: And disappointing. Is it disappointing also?

P: No. I couldn't say that yet. I'd have to say that at the end rather than now.

HS: I'm just asking so far. You're not disappointed so far that you're not less than totally panicked.

P: Oh no, I feel at this point that in my life as a person and as an actress I should be able to deal with being in public circumstances.

HS: You suddenly bring in your whole life, your being a person, your being an actress.

P: Yes.

HS: I'm supposed to take to the hills or what is my cue on that one?

P: I don't know. [*Laughing nervously*]

HS: Or is the entire audience supposed to leave the room?

P: No, no. I'm saying that I'm not as panicked as I expected to be because I don't know, because I've been alive for so many years, and I'm an actress.

HS: [*Interrupting*] I notice that I suddenly had the fantasy of smashing you across the side of the head. Has that ever happened to you? [*Looking at her directly and intently, and said in a completely dry matter of fact tone*]

P: Uh . . . [*Looks up and away*]

HS: With my fist, specifically.

P: I think it's happened to me with a hand, not with a fist.

HS: With a hand.

P: Yeah.

HS: Did the hand, did not belong to anyone evidently?

These are the first three minutes of this interview. In the course of this interview, which is slightly longer than one hour, Searles will go on to tell the patient a variety of reactions that he has to her, some of which are intensely aggressive and violent images. The filmed interview inevitably makes professional audiences uncomfortable or even distressed, although it also elicits a variety of other reactions to be discussed soon. Here, we selected just a few comments that emphasize Searles' expression of his own fantasies, and in this incidence in particular, we focus on his directly aggressive expressions. But first, let's briefly examine what we have observed thus far in the first three minutes of the interview.

Within seconds, literally within a heartbeat, Searles tunes into the patient's mention of her heart beating. Consciously, she was referring to a feeling of anxiety, her heart beating. Searles, however, does not miss the opportunity to wonder with her if she is quite sure that she is alive. Now, of course, we might dismiss this as Searles' own obsessional preoccupation with matters of aliveness and deadness, and the patient does in fact dismiss it by referring to R. D. Laing's existential concerns as stereotyped textbook explanations. Perhaps, given the aggression that Searles will quickly unleash at the patient, we might also speculate that his concern with life and death reflects his own murderous rage toward the patient. And yet, at least for some viewers of the video, there is a sense that Searles' persistence is an effort to break through the patient's sealed-off defensiveness and to find a way to make contact with her deadened and deadening selves. Searles immediately looks dejected and disappointed. It seems to us that he was inviting his patient to play with him along the lines of, "Okay, you refer to your heart beating, can you play with me about this reflecting your concern about being alive?" Searles is dejected that his patient refuses to engage, and he lets her know it. His aggression, however, is quickly unleashed more directly than many of us would imagine. He tells her frankly that he pictures himself hitting her in the head. He pauses momentarily, and then adds, as if for dramatic effect, "with my fist, specifically." When she responds that she has been hit but by a hand and not a fist, Searles grabs onto this response as an indication that she is functioning on the level of part-objects and dissociation—that is, it is not a full or identifiable person who has hit her, but a hand or a fist disconnected from a fully human being. Within seconds, we have been taken to a scene of intense aggression, sado-masochism, part-object relating in the paranoid-schizoid position, and dehumanization and dissociation—all with a patient whom he has just met and knows almost nothing about. He is engaging, or attempting to engage, her in an enactment of what he intuits are her dynamic issues, and sure enough, we do later learn that she engages her husband in sado-masochistic, violent fights in which blood is indeed drawn. Once again, as Sawyer (2011) warned us in the first case, to an outsider the interview might well seem both bizarre and inappropriate. In this case, does he reach and connect with the patient? We only have Searles' recorded reactions and unfortunately do not have the patient's feedback, as it seems no effort was made to debrief or interview her to determine her experience of the interview, and so this is left for us to speculate about.

Searles (1979) notes that in doing hospital and public interviews, one's relationship with the audience is often more challenging than that with the patient. He notes that audiences often have mixed responses, both admiring him and also reacting somewhat shocked, angered, and mystified by some of his responses to patients. He notes on several occasions that it is very difficult for him when the audience is not on his side, and he feels that he is the crazy one, the abusive, sadistic, non-human monster, while the patient is viewed as sane, gentle, and vulnerable, devoid of sadism and hatefulness. Searles' dramatic presentations, his quick use of self-disclosure, and his immediate focus on life and death, the human and the inanimate, were exaggerated, even extreme, and lent themselves to splitting.

Having shown this video and others of Searles to a wide range of professional audiences, we can certainly say that the reactions are mixed, with individuals having an assortment of reactions, but more often the responses are split. Some detest the interviewing, feeling that Searles is simply a sadistic misogynistic brute, while others admire and deeply envy his profound insight, courage in displaying his personal reactions and pathology, and expertise in utilizing these subjective reactions to make contact with difficult patients. Remember that even Sawyer, who credits Searles with changing her life in a single interview, also had an earlier interview with him in which she thought he was an uncomprehending jerk. This is another good example of how Searles managed to induce splitting in those around him, loving him or hating him, admiring him or detesting him, wishing that after sufficient analysis one could be like him in his spontaneous use of his subjectivity or else feeling that he was a sadistic and exhibitionistic abuser. We believe that this splitting, so common a reaction to watching Searles, is a direct reflection of his personality and his clinical methodology, which consists of exaggeration, dramatization, and specifically the staging of internal object relations, particularly primitive aggressive object relations so often ignored or deflected by psychotherapists.

As Akhtar (2007) mentions when referring to Masud Khan, when it comes to the work of controversial figures there is a splitting in the readers' response (see also Hopkins & Kuchuck, in press). He warns us that we always need to manage our harsh superego response, shame and anxiety, our devaluation and criticism. Here, we would like to add the other side of what is split off, which is the admiration and idealization for those exciting controversial figures who could dare do what we renounce and who express our own forbidden desire.

Cigars and electric chairs

Some brief exchanges as the interview continues. Searles is smoking a cigar, and P tells him that her father smokes too. Searles asks her whether she likes watching her father kill himself like that (19 minutes into the interview):

HS: You're just not the violent type. Humm?
P: I like to think of myself as passive, but I don't know if I am.
HS: Again, I then had some urge to get up, grab you by the hair, smash your head into the wall. Some feeling of let's get

through this [*clashing his hands in fists back and forth for emphasis*], to use a psychoanalytic expression for the moment, shit, let's get through this shit.

P: [*Laughing and smiling*] Do you have those feelings with all of your patients?

Later (33 minutes into interview):

HS: You pretend to be puzzled better than anybody I know.

P: I'm not pretending. I'm not sure what you're asking me all the time. Or what you're saying.

HS: I can't tell for sure though unless I draw blood, I thought of cutting you, to be sure that it's real. Huh?

P: To what?

HS: To be sure if it's real. I wouldn't know if you are pretending or not, unless I cut you, and if I could see the blood then I'd know there was something real there.

P: Would you feel? Is that how you feel? I mean you're saying you would have to draw blood to . . .

HS: Is that how I feel or is that how you feel? Huh?

P: That's not how I feel.

HS: You don't have any urge to draw blood to see if the other person, as they say, is real? Humm?

Later in the interview, Searles asks the patient what she imagines her mother would be saying if she were there at the interview, sitting in that chair. Later (54 minutes), Searles associates to this question as follows:

HS: When I asked if, what if your mother were sitting in that chair, I thought of an electric chair, does that get back to why you wouldn't want to do me in or something?

P: An electric chair?

HS: You've never heard of an electric chair?

P: Yes [*enunciating in an exaggeratedly clear manner*], I have heard of an electric chair.

HS: Why do you behave as if you have never heard the phrase?

P: It's not that I was reacting to that, I was reacting to the image. I mean, how did you get to an electric chair?

HS: I don't know, when I thought of, I suppose that it was, my impression was actually, when I asked what if your mother was sitting in that chair, see.

P: Yes.

HS: And I thought of an electric chair, see, okay.

P: Umhumm.

HS: [*Now pointing directly at P and poking his hand at her repeatedly with emphasis*] I don't know how I got to it, but what it suggested to me was that I must have been and must be at that point, hating you more than I realized I was.

P: [*Looking at him intently*] So you wanted to see me [*now pointing her finger at herself*] in an electric chair.

HS: Sounds so, doesn't it! Yes. Not just see you in one, but I like things to be functional. [*P smiles and then both of them laugh and audience joins in*]

We selected these quotations from a fairly lengthy interview to give you a graphic sense of how directly aggressive Searles could be, and how much he might articulate his violent fantasies to his patients. Again, we have noticed how this very intensity can create splitting in his audiences, even decades after the event took place. Searles makes two comments in his discussion of the case that we want to highlight. The first is that when the interview was over and the patient saw Searles in the hallway, she came over to him to say goodbye and without hesitating he quite naturally put his arm around her. He tells us that at that moment he hoped many people were watching so that he would feel redeemed that he had in fact made some good contact with the young woman. The second remark was made at the very end of Searles' talk to the professionals about the interview, almost as an aside and afterthought. He tells the audience that in fact he has a daughter the patient's age and that she too is an actress. Clearly, Searles brought to this interview a variety of deep feelings that he had about his own only daughter.

We end our discussion of this videotaped teaching interview with one more story. Searles was smoking his cigar throughout much of the interview, and when he spoke to the patient about the cigar, she asked him if she could have a puff. Searles spent some time asking her about whether her father would allow her to have a drag of his cigar. When one of us (LA) first met Searles' daughter, Sandra Dickinson, an actress now in her 60s, they sat down for lunch to get to know each other and to discuss her father's life and work. The first question that he asked her was what was her favorite childhood memory of her father, who at the time was elderly but still alive. Without hesitation, Sandra replied that it was of sitting next to her father as he smoked and her taking puffs of his cigar. At the time, Sandra had not seen this video, nor had any of his children watched his work. Having been teaching Searles' work and repeatedly showing and watching this video, Aron found this to be an intensely moving story.

Searles' use of his subjectivity as an analyst

Searles was famous for these live teaching interviews that we have sampled, and he traces his own exhibitionism back to his childhood admiration for his father, who was a fabulous story and joke teller. His father owned a clothing store, and Harold grew up living just above the shop so that he spent quite a lot of time sitting in his father's store, watching, observing, and identifying with him as he told jokes and stories to his customers. Harold says that he was way too young to be listening to these racist, misogynistic, anti-Semitic jokes and stories, but he was in awe of his father, who was funny, entertaining, colorful, and smart, even though also suspicious, hostile, paranoid, and painfully depressed and psychosomatically disabled. Additionally, his father would use Harold as a model to exhibit the new clothing in the store, and so Harold's exhibitionism came to him from early on in multiple relations to his father (Langs & Searles, 1980).

Searles' mother was also dramatic in her depressions and in the extent of her brutal violence toward Harold. Searles (1979) describes his mother's abusive relationship graphically:

My often terrifyingly raging mother made life hell for me much of the time in her kitchen and environs, where I cowered like a frightened animal in a corner at the end of an alley under her cook-stove, a refuge where I could be near her but where she could not readily get at me.

(pp. 482–483)

One can see in this description the classic dilemma of an abused child, who both desperately needs his attachment figure and needs to be close to her to soothe himself from the abuse that she herself is inflicting, thus the same object who is the abuser is also needed as the attachment figure. It should not be surprising that this constellation, which is so often associated with disorganized attachment, left Searles to struggle with fears of his own violence and murderous tendencies, with a lifelong difficulty controlling his temper, suicidal thoughts, and with areas of dissociation. We provide some of these glimpses into his personal background because we think that it helps to explain how it came about that Searles was so naturally gifted at the theatrical and dramatic, and also gives some sense of how he came to have such an intuitive grasp of severe psychopathology and especially a focus on primitive aggression and violence, sado-masochism, and matters of life and death.

What is outstanding in Searles' writing and work is his remarkable ability to be candid about his own troubled experiences, and his deep self-reflection on his emotional life and its impact on him as a therapist, as well as on his patients. Searles does not try to repress or overly control his own sadism as most therapists might do; rather, in regard to a patient whose own mother used to beat the hell out of her, he wrote, "I have become more interested in the technical problem of how to beat the hell out of her in a sublimated and psychoanalytically effective fashion" (1979, p. 529). He goes on to say that there are times in his teaching interviews "when I have had the delightful experience of the patient and myself as being two subjectively diabolical sadists fully enjoying ourselves in childlike playfulness which clearly is doing both of us a great deal of good" (p. 535).

The question, of course, is what does Searles mean? How does a therapist enact violence toward a patient in a way that is therapeutic, analytic, or beneficial? We believe that there was a method to Searles' madness, and that the dramatic or dramatological point of view is necessary to explain it.

Decades before relationalists formulated "multiple-self theory," Searles spoke in the language of multiple selves, dual-identity, dissociation, jealousy, and envy of internal objects. For example, Searles spoke of "multiple identity processes," the "myriad persons" (internal objects) within a person's internal world (1979, p. 460). Searles admits to feeling jealous of the patient's relations with other figures or characters in their inner world. He says that one way he knows a person is multiple is because he feels "outnumbered" by a group or tribe of these introjects (1979, 470). Searles was particularly critical of American ego psychology precisely because he believed that ego psychologists were overly enthralled with the concept of identity:

> I have come to see that the healthy individual's sense of identity is far from being monolithic in nature. It involves rather, myriad internal objects functioning in lively and harmonious interaction . . . but does not involve their being congealed into so unitary a mass as I once thought.
>
> (1979, p. 462)

Searles' advocacy of multiplicity anticipates such writers of contemporary relational theory as Bromberg (1998a), who has been the leading contemporary exponent of multiple self-states. For Bromberg, just as we have seen for Searles,

> the normal human mind is not a unitary configuration. Rather, it is defined by nonlinear, discontinuous states of consciousness that attain a coherence that overrides the awareness of discontinuity and leads to the experience of a cohesive sense of personal identity and the healthy illusion of being "one self."
>
> (Bromberg, 1998b, p. 228)

Searles' critique of ego psychology's championing of ego-identity, as well as his clinical monitoring of the subtle shifts in his own subjectivity, is remarkably similar to Bromberg's contemporary theoretical and clinical formulations. We emphasize that Searles anticipated the contemporary relational focus on multiplicity and multiple self-states precisely because Searles' technique centered on his bringing up on the analytic stage all of the patient's and his own multiple selves and giving them voices in a dramatic engagement— and remember that for Searles' live interviews, it was usually quite literally a stage performance.

Searles argued that especially in the treatment of more seriously disturbed patients, it is necessary for the analyst to acknowledge their emotional connection to the patient. Searles is an advocate of a much deeper and far more frankly acknowledged feeling-involvement with patients than what is acceptable in a classical analysis. He came to the conclusion that to the degree that an analysis is "rigorously classical, it is essentially delusional" (1979, p. 458). By "rigorously classical" Searles meant that it preserved the analyst as neutral, non-feeling, and therefore non-human, where all of the pathology was thought to reside in the patent. To the contrary, he believed that the more human analysts showed themselves to be, the more patients could use the analyst as a human model of feelingfulness. Still, he did not advocate that all therapists do it the way he did, but rather that their own personal analyses have gotten them far enough so that they could be in good touch with their own emotional lives rather than try to eliminate their emotional reactions.[3] The importance of the analyst's access to all of their emotional reactions and states is pervasive in Searles' work (1960, 1965, 1979, 1986, and see Langs & Searles, 1980).

We want to turn our attention toward what was called "paradigmatic therapy," an approach to psychoanalytic therapy that Searles appreciated and which he himself influenced but was also influenced by, even while he remained critical of some of its features. We think it is worth this detour because in some striking ways paradigmatic therapy has similarities to the dramatic or dramaturgic point of view that we have described throughout this book. We will first describe paradigmatic therapy and then explain Searles' reservations about it, because we think that his concerns are justified, and the depiction, along with his criticisms, serves to sharpen our own arguments.

Marie Coleman Nelson and her colleagues (1968) created an approach to psychoanalytic therapy based on the enactment of various roles by the therapist to resolve resistances and promote maturational growth. Nelson and her colleagues were associated with the National Psychological Association for Psychoanalysis (NPAP) as well as with Hyman Spotnitz and Modern Psychoanalysis. Nelson was theoretically Freudian but attempting to develop a more active technique especially applicable to borderline and pre-Oedipal patients. It is fascinating to realize that as early as the 1950s and 60s, she was inspired to develop this approach by the case vignette with which we started this book—that of Ferenczi playing the role of grandpapa.

Anticipating much of the contemporary postmodern focus on multiplicity and the relational conceptualization of multiple self-states, Nelson understood individuals as being composed of multiple selves. Her image for this multiple self-structure is one that we find quite evocative. She pictures these selves as parallel to one another, like strings on a harp, with one or several more prominent at any one time. The goal of the paradigmatic therapy is one of harmonious functioning among the various selves.

The therapist accomplishes this goal by dramatizing the role the patient plays, exaggerating it, mirroring it. In paradigmatic treatment, the analyst is thought to enact different roles, which are induced by various ego states of the analysand. At times, the therapist supports or mirrors the resistance of the patient rather than interpreting it, sides with the patient, or becomes the antagonist whom the patient must defeat, assuming the role of the hostile introject.

Nelson, who was known for her acerbic wit, illustrates this with the tale of a patient who received a raise. He had the feeling that he should pay the therapist more, but he also wanted to use the money for other things. The patient agonized over the issue: "Should I or shouldn't I?" Nelson's response: "Give it all to me!"

The paradigmatic approach was often criticized for disrupting the transference, but Nelson argued that exaggerating or dramatizing the transference was useful because the patient could then see it more strikingly. Yet she also argued that it need not involve dramatic activity, even though she herself tended to speak dramatically about it! She said, "Actually it can be a very laid-back thing. It doesn't have to manifest with fireworks" (Molino, 1996, p. 74).

Turning to Searles' reactions and critique, Searles was clearly impressed with the clinical flexibility and innovativeness of the approach and referred to it repeatedly. In addition, he approved of the critique of the reliance on interpretation as the exclusive tool of the analyst. He was critical, however, that the therapist was presented as acting in an "artificial" manner, which he considered "degrading to the essential uniqueness and emotional profundity of any human being" (1968–1969, p. 698). Searles argued that the deliberate, non-natural role-playing lent itself to the analyst's defensiveness and grandiosity, and in any event was unnecessary as therapists always already have the full range of self-states available to them as part of their genuine emotional reactions.

> As I see it, the patient can find a real sample of every conceivable kind, or combination of kinds, of feelings and attitudes in the therapist. The therapist may function with immense helpfulness to the patient in utilizing this or that sample of his own real self (whether it be a "crazy" sample, a stupid sample, or whatever), but it is not all play-acting.
>
> (p. 699)

Searles thought that role-playing, enactment, and dramatization were essential, but like all "corrective emotional experiences" they should be evoked naturally and authentically without need for feigned emotional performances.

As we have noted, Searles elicited, and his writings and videos continue to evoke, intense reactions from his readers and audiences. He is loved and admired and envied by some, and seen as a misogynistic, out-of-control, sadistic brute by others. In short, Searles evokes splitting in his spectators. He was, as we have seen, a natural performer, and he knew how to play to the audience and elicit strong affective reactions. It is therefore easy to idealize him as a brilliant clinician who pioneered the treatment of borderline and schizophrenic patients and who could reach those regarded as unreachable by using access to his own subjectivity with unparalleled mastery. Similarly, it is easy to dismiss him as a showman who took advantage of his reputation to exhibit himself at his patients' expense. We have regularly heard both portrayals. What should also be said is that Searles himself was quite aware of, and directly discussed, both sets of reactions. Of course, it troubled him when people suggested that he was sicker than the psychotic patients he was interviewing. Nevertheless, Searles insisted that the way to teach psychotherapy was by doing psychiatric interviews live, in front of an audience, or recording the consultations and having students and colleagues carefully observe them. He knew that most therapists would never take the risk of so exposing themselves, and he prided himself on his doing so. We do not think that what ultimately matters is how people react to Searles' personality, but rather that Searles' work opens the door to important questions with which we continue to struggle. What a goldmine of clinical data, observations, and clinical formulations and challenges he has left us.

To work effectively as a psychoanalyst requires that the clinician trust in her spontaneous reactions and maintain a sense of confidence in the use of her subjectivity, in the unconscious, so to speak. And yet, we all have good reason not to trust ourselves too much. Searles himself pointed out, for example, that just when a therapist might think that he was playing the role of the patient's father, he might very well be defending against playing the role of the patient's mother. Just when we think we are being a "good" object, this may be when we are being most hurtful. One of the great paradoxes of psychoanalysis is that analysts must trust themselves quite a bit to do this work with any spontaneity and freedom, but must also question themselves and be suspicious about their own motivations. Searles was aware of his tendency toward aggression, as well as his capacity for love, jealousy, envy, and a wide range of feelings, and what he struggled with, and left as a legacy, is the question of how to make use of all his many selves, including those often dismissed as crazy or sadistic or exploitative. How do you beat a patient up, since it is unavoidable that you will do so, in a way that is constructive and therapeutic, he often wondered? Sedgwick (1993) argued that Searles' clinical approach elucidated Jung's theoretical positions, even though Searles himself had not read much of Jung's writings and rarely referred to Jung. One commonality is that Jung, like Searles, thought that therapists could be "too nice." Jung thought that the therapist needed to be devilish. Jung wrote, and Searles concurs, that a therapist needs "a certain amount of cruelty" (Jung, quoted in Sedgwick, p. 125).

Here we would like to make the link between Searles' work and Bion and the post-Bionians' approach. Both analysts were focused on living something with a patient rather than on giving rational explanations and interpretations. In different ways, they both focused on exploring levels of truth in the analytic encounter and emphasized the value of such contact with the patient and with parts of themselves. Ogden (2007a) argues that "Searles is without peer in demonstrating what that need for truth looks like and feels like in the transference-countertransference, and how it shapes the analytic experience . . ." (p. 336), and notes, "I have found that reading Searles provides a vibrant clinical context for Bion's work and that reading Bion provides a valuable theoretical context for Searles' work" (p. 365). In our words, Bion dreamt a brilliant theory that Searles lived clinically. Searles had developed his clinical approach independently, even though later in his career he appreciated Bion and recognized an affinity with the British group. Both men, from different theoretical backgrounds and from different parts of the world, held similar sensibilities: Bion mostly via abstract theory and Searles mostly through clinical demonstration.

As we discussed in the previous chapter, Ferro's approach emphasizes bringing all the "characters" of the analytic field to life in the analysis so that they can be transformed. Following Bion, Ferro focuses on how the analyst contains and metabolizes the patient's undigested material and feeds these back to the patient in digestible forms such that the patient learns to digest or alphabetize. Consider the similarity of Searles emphasizing the patient's "innumerable personalities" that exist in an "undigested" state (1965, p. 60n) and which he helps them process and develop.

Our conceptualization of contemporary clinical practice featuring dramatic dialogue makes use of this common theme: the analyst's facilitating the emergence of multiple selves, characters, internal objects, onto the analytic stage where in scene after scene they are lived, articulated, developed, processed, and transformed. Generative enactment thus becomes not just an occasional mishap, but the *modus operandi* of psychoanalysis.

Notes

1 Personal communication from Anita Sawyer to Lewis Aron, February 22, 2017. We wish to thank Anita Sawyer for her feedback on this summary of her personal story.
2 The authors wish to express enormous gratitude to Clemens Loew, PhD, for providing a copy of the tape of this interview for educational use. We are also deeply indebted to Donald Searles, Harold's son, for providing permission on behalf of the Searles family for the use of these historically invaluable materials.
3 From his very first article, written in 1948–1949 while he was just beginning his analytic training and before completing his residency, Searles argued that transference reactions were not distortions but rather that all transference manifestations have some real basis in the analyst's behavior. (See a reprint of this first article in *Psychoanalytic Dialogues*, along with an introduction to Searles' work; Aron & Lieberman, 2017). This radical critique of the blank screen position (Hoffman, 1983) represented a fully constructivist, interactional point of view, decades before Merton Gill made this point the basis for his radical critique of psychoanalysis in the late 1970s.

Chapter 7

At-one-ment, mutual vulnerability, and co-suffering

This chapter elaborates a model of "at-one-ment," featuring mutual vulnerability and shared suffering as significant aspects of therapeutic action. It describes the "dance party," which brings onto the analytic stage multiple self-states of both analyst and patient. At-one-ment is understood as becoming at one with the present moment of the field. It refers to the creation of a shared regulatory system, sometimes called thirdness or the analytic third, achieved through mutual surrender, a joint dance toward expansion that facilitates the generative use of subjectivity. The chapter highlights and weaves together aspects of mind, body, and spirit.

The dramatic dialogue model assumes that we live with our patients their psychic and relational reality by becoming one with it in the present moment (Bion, 1970). In that process, we are not separated from one another but unconsciously interwoven, as we live together undigested and inchoate emotional moments, and formulate them by living them through, enacting, with each character playing out a scene. The patient then is the lead actor who unconsciously invites and recruits the analyst to play necessary parts in a dramatic enactment on the psychoanalytic stage.

To support this perspective, in this chapter we revisit the dialectics of Enigmatic and Pragmatic, old and new, as well as action and reflection. We discuss drama as dreaming, and the notion of suffering with another person as we become at-one with the drama of their psychic and relational reality. Using Ogden's (2015) reading of Bion, we discuss the intuitive ways in which we live relational and psychic truth with our patients, strive to stay alive, recognize ourselves and our participation in our mind and body, look inside and outside, and as Levenson (1985) suggested, ask not only what does it mean, but wonder, "what's going on around here?" We re-introduce the metaphor of the "dance party," where the analyst brings into that drama her own characters; only then can the "party" begin.

We open by turning our attention to Bion, who privileged intuition and learning from experience over rational clinical inferences, and who elaborated this through the concept of "at-one-ment." Bion (1970) makes clear that "at-one-ment" is not only a religious or mystical notion, but a fundamental assumption of science and psychoanalysis. It occurs regularly in our dreaming, both when asleep and in waking dreaming, reverie, as we are at-one with the reality of our dreams. When we are at-one with our unconscious emotional lives, we are most ourselves, most real to ourselves. Reverie, for Bion, is the analyst's way of being at-one with "O," which in this context is the psychic reality of the moment in the analysis.

Bion's writing on at-one-ment is usefully compared with that of Hans Loewald. Loewald (1979) wrote of making "at-one-ment" alluding to atonement, the intimate connection between repentance and self-sacrifice. Loewald developed a psychoanalytic vision of the origin of mind in which at the start, and in the deep unconscious, there is no differentiation between inside and outside, self and other, fantasy and actuality, past and present. As Mitchell (2000) explained Loewald's theory, all of these dichotomies, which we take for granted as the given features of the world, are for Loewald complex constructions that arise out of an original primal density. The primal density of unconscious life, lack of differentiation, at-one-ment, underlies the later differentiations and bounded structures that make rational, secondary process thinking and adult functioning possible. Keeping Loewald's theory in mind helps us remain aware that while we are thinking of patients and ourselves as separate and distinct individuals, simultaneously, in another register, we are interconnected, at-one-with, undifferentiated.

To the ideas of "becoming-at-one" and "at-one-ment," we want to add attention to Harold Searles' notion of "therapeutic symbiosis," an idea he proposed as early as 1958 and developed throughout his career (see especially Searles, 1965, 1979, 1986). The analyst must come to accept a transitional-object or an even more deeply symbiotic degree of transference relatedness. What Searles means is that therapists need to accept their mutually dependent relationship with the patient. Because the therapeutic process occurs within the dyadic system rather than in the individual, both the patient and the analyst emerge out of this symbiosis with an enhanced sense of individuation, personal growth. Much like Kohut's (1971) later notion of the self-object, which also refers to the experience of the other as part of the self, each of these formulations is speaking of a register in which the analyst becomes therapeutically and generatively at-one with the patient by joining as part of the analytic third or analytic field.

While Ogden (2015) understands reverie as an intersubjective phenomenon, nevertheless he suggests that the way the analyst enters a state of reverie is by engaging "in an act of self-renunciation" (p. 294). Self-renunciation is defined as

> the act of allowing oneself to become *less definitively oneself* in order to create a psychological space in which analyst and patient may enter into a shared state of intuiting and being-at-one-with a disturbing psychic reality that the patient, on his own, is un-able to bear.
>
> (p. 294, emphasis added)

It is regarding his understanding of "self-renunciation" as essential to reverie that we wish to amend Ogden's formulation. Ogden explains that renunciation allows the analyst to be "less definitively oneself" (p. 294) as a means of becoming at-one with the patient's psychic reality. Here, Ogden is using a notion of the analyst's self as singular, one-self; one is (more or less) oneself. Since he starts with the notion of the singular or unified self, he can only formulate becoming at-one with the patient's psychic reality as a matter of "self-renunciation." In contrast, throughout this book, we emphasize the notion of multiplicity or multiple self-state theory. Since we begin with the assumption that the analyst's mind is structured along the lines of multiple self-states, becoming at-one with the psychic reality of the session is not conceived as involving renunciation so much as a *generative use of the therapist's subjectivity* that requires surrender. Analysts' use of their subjectivity involves the free-floating access to and generative use of the wide range of self-states elicited by or evoked in the session at any moment. Some of these states may be differentiated and defined, whereas other self-states are less differentiated or even merged. In becoming a character in the patient's narrative, we are at-one with the patient's unconscious psychic reality. Without seeking to, we surrender and take on a role in the theater of the unconscious as we are dreaming up the patient's world.

As an alternative to Loewald's speaking of "sacrifice" and Ogden's language of "self-renunciation," we suggest that Ghent's (1990) term "surrender" may better capture the bi-directional analytic process. Surrender, according to Ghent, may look like submission, but whereas submission, like resistance, is anti-growth, a masochistic giving oneself up to another, surrender is a force toward growth. Surrender is a process of letting down one's guard and one's defenses and requires faith in the sense elaborated by Eigen (1981), a creative way of experiencing with one's whole being.

For Ghent, surrender reflected a basic human need to expand and liberate the self through surrendering to the new and the unknown, to transformation and transcendence (Suchet, 2016, Roth, 2017), faith in the possibility of repair, faith in the possibility of growth, faith in the possibility of reaching emotional truth.

Benjamin's (2004) most widely read article, "Beyond Doer and Done-to," builds on Ghent's distinction. Benjamin argues that the key point was that surrender is not to someone. Rather than submitting to another, the person lets go into being fully with the other, implying the idea of mutual recognition. From this source, Benjamin infers the necessity of the third, a principle or process that mediates between self and other. Patient and analyst surrender to the third, to a process and principle larger than either of them, and one which entails a shared vulnerability and co-suffering, in the faith that it will lead to repair, growth, and transformation.

The emphasis of the phrase "becoming-at-one" is on the verb "becoming," which signifies enactment rather than only observation, understanding, or insight. Becoming-at-one suggests transformation and generative enactment. The term "becoming" is associated with Bion's writings. While not generally referring to or making use of the term "intersubjectivity," as Brown (2011) points out, the Kleinian and Bionian literature contains an implicit intersubjective theory that describes how the analyst must become an aspect of the patient and how that becoming may lead to a process of transforming unconscious and/or unrepresented experience by dreaming together. Brown (2011) quotes Gabriel García Márquez, who wrote: "In the end, it is impossible not to become what others believe you are" (p. 673), which conveys the inevitability and clinical necessity of analysts and patients each identifying with what is projected into them. In their use of projective identification as a form of unconscious communication, the Klein/Bion theorists recognize that the patient's inner world is brought to life in the analysis as a total situation (Joseph, 1985). "It seems necessary for the patient that *the analyst should become involved in the living out* of some aspects of phantasies that reflect his internal object relations" (Feldman, 1997, p. 228, emphasis added).[1]

The analyst plays the character assigned to him by the patient's unconscious daimon/director. Bach (2016), building on Kohut and his self-object concept, says that analysts wear the suits made for them by their patients. Bach recalls an incident described in Kohut's (1971) early work, in which a patient idealized his analyst as "just like" the priest to whom he confessed as a child. Uncomfortable with "the suit that the patient gave him," this analyst had told the patient that he was not a Catholic, thus rejecting the costume of the priest's collar and handing it back to the patient. It is quite like the language of contemporary self psychology and systems theory, where the analyst is described as "wearing the attribute" imposed on them by patients (Lichtenberg, Lachmann, & Fosshage, 1996, p. 11). As we discuss later, when invited to a dance party one needs to dress for the occasion.

Bion distinguishes between the "K" and "O" links, where "K" signifies knowledge *about* the analysand, derived from listening to free associations and then making inferences about its meanings. The more intuitive and direct way of knowing a patient is to become or be "at-one" with "O," the emerging emotional truth of the session (Bion, 1970, p. 33). As we have elaborated throughout the book, a contemporary psychoanalytic approach emphasizes experience along with insight, intuition, and awareness, becoming along with understanding, dreaming up, enacting, dramatizing, and interpreting. Here, we emphasize not only understanding but the notion of being at-one with, which involves surrendering and co-suffering.

Grotstein (2009), also building on Bion, believes that viewing psychoanalysis as a dramatic enactment constitutes a paradigm shift in theory that could only happen once we shifted from a purely one-person to a field theory or two-person psychology. The expansion of psychoanalytic theory beyond a purely intrapsychic one-person psychology is expressed in the language of a two-person or inter-subjective psychology, a field theory or systems theory, and in the notion of a psychoanalytic dialogue or dramatic dialogue. He wrote, "It is my belief, consequently, that drama constitutes the fundamental function of the psychoanalytic scene" (p. 190). The psychoanalytic session, viewed more deeply, is constituted as an ongoing theatrical play or novel that is enacted on the psychoanalytic stage.

Grotstein weaves these ideas into his understanding of Bion's late contributions, while building on the well-articulated descriptions of Joyce McDougall (see Chapter 3). He understands dramatization as analogous with Bion's conception of dreaming. The dramatic enactment constitutes a mutual dreaming of the patient's psychic themes. Patient and analyst dream together, a dramatic dream, conflicted, interactive, elaborating in staged scenes the patient's unmetabolized emotions, self-states, and undeveloped internal objects. On one hand, the play is performed spontaneously and improvisationally (Ringstrom, 2001), but behind this appearance, according to Grotstein, there is an unconscious ventriloquist, a daimon, or dramaturge that initiates and is the creator of the play. In this description, the analytic stage, or theater, is equivalent to the analytic field or, put differently, the analytic field may be understood as the executive producer of the analytic passion play. The idea of "becoming one" with something invites analyst and patient to the same stage to dream a mutual dream and live together the past and the future, as they appear in the present moment.

"In dreaming, we are not dreaming *about* something, we are *dreaming something*, 'dreaming up' an aspect of ourselves. In dreaming, we are *at-one* with the *reality* of the dream; we are the dream" (Ogden, 2015, p. 294). In the same way, on the analytic stage, we are not playing *about* something, we are playing something that we become. We are ourselves in the most real and genuine way; our mind and body as well as our own internal objects and dissociative selves are present participants in the intrapsychic and intersubjective drama. "At-one-ment" or "becoming-at-one" or "therapeutic symbiosis" may all seem mystical and enigmatic, if not outright psychotic. We are not denying that they indeed may be. But there is also a Pragmatic dimension, as those are ways of describing becoming part of a regulatory system greater than yourself and larger than the patient, a system that includes both self- and mutual regulation and is greater than the sum of its parts. One plus one makes three, an analytic third.[2] The metaphors of playing, dramatizing, dancing, and dreaming with the patient are all ways of describing how the analyst joins with the patient in a system of mutual regulation, and enactment is generative precisely because it serves to influence this dyadic system from within, from the inside out.

Taking into consideration the notion of multiplicity, in the psychoanalytic dialogue the analyst tolerates the inevitable contact between the patient's internal objects and parts of the self, and her own split-off parts of the self and internal objects—what we refer to as the "dance party." In that dialogue, we believe that the analyst is not only a participant, but ideally also serves as a container for it. The analyst holds the physical and emotional tension that is part of the intensity of every unconscious dialogue: the pain and anxiety that every true intimate interaction evokes, and especially the pain that the specific role the analyst is playing elicited. The analytic function then is not necessarily action oriented in a visible, Pragmatic way, but includes hidden and Enigmatic enactments, the ability to contain, regulate, and even suffer, perhaps especially suffer.

The dancing party

Dramatic dialogue, as we have proposed, is based on ideas of multiplicity and dissociated self-states in both analyst and patient. Ferenczi comes to see the analytic engagement as an inevitable, mutual participation and recreation of the childhood histories and particularly of the pathogenic traumas of both the patient and the analyst. In his investigations of mutuality, he deconstructed the polarized dichotomies of word/deed, association/interpretation, transference/countertransference, and patient/analyst. As we have seen in Chapter 3, Ferenczi argued that the analyst and patient participate together in a drama, a dramatic reliving, moving beyond the narrow confines of verbal exchange. Mitchell, as we examined in Chapter 4, utilized the metaphor of dancing with the patient to highlight their joint participation and progressive mutual attunement. Most recently, Benjamin (2018) speaks of patients and analysts as caught in symmetrical dance steps, "finding a dance partner," rhythmic patterns of dance. Benjamin emphasizes the metaphor of dance to capture aspects of symmetry within rigid complementary relations, as well as breaking out of such rigid patterns into looser movement, the "dance of thirdness." For Mitchell, Benjamin, Slavin and Rahmani (2016), and for us, dance captures the spirit of enactment and play in its Winnicottian meaning, a squiggle game of mutual participation, rhythmicity, recognition, and thirdness.

Living with the patient her early trauma, and playing out not only her dissociated parts but also her early objects, is painful, especially when those were disappointing, traumatizing, or abusive. Encouraging analysts to be good new objects is a relief to many of us, since it prevents the pain that playing the bad parts of the object causes the analyst, especially since we already carry our own bad internal objects and have complicated relationships with them. What happens then when our internal objects get on the stage together with the patient's objects? Whose bad objects are they, as Davies (2004) asks? What does a dance party of bad objects look like?

Imagine the patient playing his internal drama, and in so doing, his bad objects appear on the analytic stage. He casts the analyst to play them. As the analyst becomes, let's say, the patient's abandoning mother, her own internal mother gets on the stage. Her mother then starts dancing with the patient's mother. Can the analyst tolerate that wild dance? Does she refuse to wear the party dress? Does she try to turn the music off, call the police to end the party? As Ferenczi describes, now the analyst is confronted with her own badness and is not allowed to deny her guilt, shame, and anxiety.

"Why do I always have to play the bad guy?" you often hear children ask. Can the analyst tolerate playing the bad object, hold the patient's, and manage her own without feeling some amount of pain? Obviously, the answer is no. It is painful to hold badness in our mind and body, and we can see how traditionally the notion of transference as displacement and distortion helped the analyst to tolerate and work through negativity. The notion of transference allows an "as if" quality; the analyst is the bad object, while believing that those parts don't really belong to her but to the original parent in the transference. Contemporary relational psychoanalysis, by reconceptualizing the notion of transference, forced analysts to own the ways in which they impact patients, and in that sense acknowledge that anything the patient observes is based on something real that the patient picks up. The move is then from an analytic model where everything is fantasy, transference, and "not real," to a relational model where everything is "too real; it is really about me and you." That contemporary perspective creates a challenge for analysts, since now playing the bad object involves intense painful feelings of guilt or shame about being a disappointing and a bad parent to the patient, a reminder of the analyst's own self-states and objects. Here, we are not dealing only with the patient's experience of the analyst as good, bad, or both, but with analysts' experiences of themselves, their (multiple) self-relations, and the painful self-recognition of less integrated shameful and guilt-ridden self-states.

Grotstein tells us that the following case is the one that most convinced him of the power of this new paradigm linking drama and dreaming. Of course, this is a brief sketch; for more details, see Grotstein (2009).

The patient was a single, 30-something-year-old physician who had been born in England during World War II. His father died in action during the war, and Grotstein frequently felt a great distance between himself and the patient, as if he were dead to him. The patient was grateful to the stepfather who had raised him and supported him through medical school. At some point, the patient began a session by telling Grotstein that there was something he needed to tell him that Grotstein did not yet know. About five years earlier, on a trip back to England to visit his grandparents, he went to a pub with his grandfather where he saw a man staring at him, and he asked his grandfather who the man was. It turned out that it was his biological father who had in fact not been killed in the war. His father told him that he and the mother made it up because the mother had become involved with a wealthy man, and they decided that it would be better for their son to be raised in privilege and with the benefits of a good education. Upon finishing this story, the patient looked at Grotstein and asked, "Will you be my father?" Without thinking, Grotstein emphatically answered that he would. (He wore the suit that the patient made for him.) The patient suddenly changed his mood and loudly cried out, asking, "Why did you do it?!" He proceeded to unleash a vitriolic attack against his father/analyst for having abandoned and betrayed him. It was at this moment that Grotstein began to wonder if in fact all analytic sessions were not theatrical en-act-ments in which he was appointed as actor in his patient's internal drama. This is remarkably like the paradigmatic illustration of the "grandpapa" with which we began this book, when Ferenczi found himself spontaneously addressing his patient in an intimate whisper playing a character role in a dramatic dialogue. Both Grotstein and Ferenczi were struck by the way they each immediately, naturally, spontaneously talked with their patients as characters in their stories.

From this perspective of session as theatrical enactment, playing the patient's early internal object isn't only inevitable but also necessary to allow the patient to relive and then work through the early injuries, trauma, and object relations. This perspective challenges the binary between old and new and assumes that not only does the old always live in the new, but that the seeds of the new exist in the old (as in the prospective function discussed in Chapter 2).

Ferenczi, in his efforts to be the "good object," realized that in fact the analyst always repeated old injuries. In a highly dramatic moment of Ferenczi's (1932) *Clinical Diary* (and it should be said that the diary has numerous dramatic moments), Ferenczi realizes that he has hurt a patient more than he had intended. In the act of interpreting, he had cruelly flung words into his patient's face. He understands that his words could have murdered. Ferenczi comes to the realization that

> it is an unavoidable task for the analyst: although he may behave as he will, he may take kindness and relaxation as far as he possibly can, the time will come when he will have to repeat with his own hands the act of murder previously perpetrated against the patient. In contrast to the original murder, however, he is not allowed to deny his guilt.
>
> (p. 52)

Ferenczi discovered that despite the best conscious intentions, it was inevitable for the analyst to reenact the old or bad object. The analyst was different from the old object only insofar as the analyst could own this act and feel sincerely sorry for it. This was an early experiential and dramaturgical model of rupture and repair, as well as what Benjamin (2009, 2018) later developed as a model of acknowledgment.

In this passage, we read Ferenczi as he discovers the inevitability of reenactment of the patient's most powerful trauma: "This hangman's work is inevitable" (p. 53), he writes. Ferenczi realizes that the enactment reengages both the patient's life history as well as his own. "This gave me an opportunity to penetrate much deeper into my own infantilism: the tragic moment in childhood when my mother declares: You are my murderer" (p. 53). Our emphasis here is not only on the patient's experiences of the analyst's subjectivity, but on what has received less attention, namely analysts' experiences of themselves, their own self-experience and self-relations, in the unavoidable reenactment of the patient's early trauma. A classic example of such difficult self-relations is that of

Davies' (2004) clinical illustration of her work with Karen, with whom Davies began to hate the version of herself that emerged in their relationship. The evocation of intensely shame-riddled bad self-representations in both patient and analyst needs to be worked through in each of them. Davies' achievement in this article is not only her brilliant theorization, but the way in which she person-ally conveys the pain and suffering that she had to bear along with Karen. Here, following Ferenczi, we emphasize the pain that the analyst inescapably experiences, the guilt, shame, and anxiety that are part of the analytic drama. Wearing an ill-fitting suit can be uncomfortable and may even pinch, and the analyst dons the outfit with only minimal protest.

Pain and suffering: Body and spirit

Let's start with an imaginary dialogue with Bion about the place of sensation and the body in psychoanalytic theory and practice, as we consider the analytic function of tolerating pain. While acting out can be a means to avoid facing the truth and bypass suffering, gen-erative enactment may be a way of bringing experience to life. Here, we would like to add the body to our discussion, breaking the binary between mind and body, and including affect regulation in our psy-choanalytic thinking (Benjamin, 2013; Benjamin & Atlas, 2015).

Ogden's (2015) reading of Bion's "Notes on Memory and Desire" (1967) implies that "the unconscious is not the realm of physical sensation. Physical sensation resides in the domain of conscious experience" (p. 292). As we understand Bion (1967, 1970), he included sensation, together with memory and desire, to be avoided as potential interferences with the analyst's "act of faith." Bion's act of faith refers to a psychoanalytic discipline that generates knowledge of rather than knowledge about. Bion was no more eschewing sensation and the body than he was eliminating memory and desire. Rather, he was attempting to separate the *a priori*, pure knowledge, knowledge of, from knowledge about, and he was concerned with analysts consciously striving after memory, willfulness, or sensation.

Bion's philosophically inspired writing is difficult and has led to much confusion, and we suggest that thinking in terms of dialectics and deconstructing binaries can help make some of those ideas clearer (Aron & Starr, 2013). To do so, we would like to emphasize here the notions of the Enigmatic and the Pragmatic (Atlas, 2015, 2016) as essential terms that help us capture the complexity of conscious–unconscious, mind–body binaries. Atlas's definition of the Enigmatic (unseen, unmeasured, metaphysical) and the Pragmatic (observed, tangible, physical) as intermingled and necessary for one another posits both as potentially related to conscious and unconscious processes. Like Meltzer and Williams' (1988) ideas about the emotional tension between the beautiful tangible mother and her enigmatic qualities and invisible insides, Atlas suggests that the Pragmatic we observe and seem to know in fact always includes Enigmatic qualities. Both Enigmatic and Pragmatic registers contain conscious and unconscious components, with consciousness embedded dialectically in unconsciousness and unconsciousness expressed in consciousness.

Rather than championing intuition at the expense of sensation, we advocate maintaining the importance of both sides of the dialectic: intuition and sensation, mind and body, knowledge of and knowledge about. Not separating mind and body means that the Pragmatic body as well as the mind yields intuition and sensation. This is in accordance with Jung's (1971) psychological types, where intuition and sensation balance each other, as do thought and feeling. As the following tale suggests, we insist on including the body in our discussion of psychoanalysis and propose that it is mind and body that is our intuitive and sensate guide to seen and hidden, known and unknown realities.

Dave, a middle-aged, successful academic whose lifestyle is determined by his regular travels on the international lecture circuit, was seeking psychotherapeutic help following what he described as two earlier, lengthy, and "reasonably helpful" periods of analyses. Dave interrupted these previous analyses knowing that he remained sufficiently symptomatic and undoubtedly needed further analysis. Still, he believed that he had gone as far as he could with each of these analysts.

Much of Dave's initial consultation was spent with him describing bodily complaints and medical illnesses including lifelong physical pain, discomfort, disease, and even more frustrating, painfully botched treatments and medical mismanagement from the time of his childhood. Indeed, one serious childhood illness had remained undiagnosed by his pediatricians until he, as a boy of 10, diagnosed himself after watching a television documentary about the disease and insisted that his doctors test him for the illness. In this first session, we spent a lot of time talking about his body, his love of massage and physical touch, his muscular awareness, tightness, pain, breathing, posture, and especially about the physical concomitants of his chronic anxiety.

In the second session, Dave began by telling me about his family and upbringing. He focused on physical abuse at the hands of older siblings and the neglectful and non-protecting responses of his parents. As he told me in some detail about his mother's lack of understanding and harshness toward him, and especially as he began to introduce me to her physical and emotional cruelty, I knew that I was finding the story to be particularly painful and sad. I was not thinking about it consciously at the time, but in retrospect, I think I felt unprepared for such a background in that the person before me seemed in many ways so successful and well-put-together. But I was only consciously aware of mild discomfort as I listened.

It was only as I reached for a sip of coffee that I noticed that I was all choked up. I wasn't sure how obvious it might have been, but it was clear to me that I could barely swallow, and for a moment I thought I'd gag on the hot liquid.

Dave showed no outward sign of noticing. I looked at him, a man in his mid-40s, a bit overweight, sitting on the edge of his chair, and said, "I'm not sure if you noticed that as I am listening, I'm feeling moved and uncomfortable by your story, but only when I caught myself on the verge of choking did I realize just how much I was feeling, more than I have let myself know."

Dave didn't skip a beat and said with tears in his eyes, "Yes, my childhood was miserable," and he began to cry. He cried just briefly and then looked at me and said, "Crying makes me feel better at times. You know, I had not felt that badly about what I was saying until I saw the look on your face. The suffering on your face touched me." He was silent for a moment and then reminded me of his illness as a child, being misdiagnosed by his physicians, "I was only 10 years old but I was the one who found out the name of the disease I had. Doctors don't actually feel your pain, so how would they know what's really going on?"

His memory was clearly a reflection of his fear, and perhaps his belief that, once again, here and now, he would be mistreated by me, but the timing of this association might also be a communication that he believed my physical symptoms, which appeared as a reaction to listening to him, would help me know his body from the inside and be able not only to diagnose him, but also to suffer with him.

While the analyst was attempting to form an affective connection with Dave, he was simultaneously laying out the framework in which he was comfortable working. Namely, it was expected that he would have all sorts of emotional, intellectual, and bodily reactions to the patient and that part of the analytic work would involve the analyst using those reactions implicitly and explicitly and being interested in the patient's experience of his presence and subjectivity (Aron, 1996).

We might think about Dave's comment as a reflection of his pathological narcissism, of his unconscious and perhaps conscious belief that he was beyond understanding by others, that he was trapped in a world of his own omnipotence. Furthermore, we can think about the analyst choking up as related to his own feelings of anxiety and fear about what the patient would do to him in the analysis. Isn't it possible that the analyst reached for his coffee just then, in reaction to his own trepidation lest the patient attack him? Is it possible that the analyst's difficulty swallowing and gagging reflected his conflict about letting Dave in or keeping him out? We could just as easily say that perhaps all the analyst did was to show that he could not appropriately handle the patient's painful affective states and that he needed to derail him from talking in greater depth about his abuse.

Was the analyst, like Dave's older brother, suggesting that the patient just shut up and stop complaining? Did Dave agree with the analyst and act as if the intervention was helpful predominantly to appease the analyst to get him to like him and back off? One way of looking at the intervention is that the analyst feels Dave is choking him, and in return he makes Dave cry, which sounds like the beginning of a brotherly brawl. If they were indeed mutually reenacting the scenario of a brotherly provocation, one might argue that the analyst already played a role resonant with his patient's internal object relations, recreating this childhood model scene, the role of his abusive brother.

We are suggesting, however, another way of hearing and understanding this childhood memory. Dave may be letting his analyst know that there are certain things he won't be able to analyze from the outside. He conveys to his analyst that only if the analyst can get inside of him, under his own skin, into his gut, will he really know him. The direction is from the inside out, then, and not from the outside-in. Here, the analyst's bodily reaction of choking on coffee may be understood as a reaction about bodies being penetrated and expelled, about one experiencing another from the inside, and in that sense it's not only a signal for the impact the patient had on the analyst, but of the analyst living in the same psychic and relational reality as the patient and becoming one with that reality. What we are describing in this clinical tale are the early stages of becoming-at-one in forming a regulatory system with the patient, an analytic third, that transcends the patient's and the analyst's individual subjectivities. Affects and states of consciousness, multiple self-states, are then regulated and continually negotiated and restructured from within this system as the system itself becomes repeatedly dysregulated and re-regulated through ongoing processes of rupture and repair. The phrase "rupture and repair" leaves out the initial stage of the process, namely, ongoing regulation, the establishment of expectancies (Beebe & Lachmann, 2002). What we are calling joining the system or establishing thirdness begins with this joining, becoming-at-one, and then is negotiated and continually transformed through ongoing cycles of rupture and repair.

For Grotstein, transference refers mostly to the transfer of mental pain from one person to another. Although he does not cite them in this context, this is the same understanding of transference utilized by both Jung and Searles. Jung (1916) views the analyst as taking on the sufferings of his patient and sharing them with him. Elsewhere, Grotstein is quite explicit about the connection between Bion and Jung, an important link that has often been "attacked" by being ignored (see, Culbert-Koehn, 1997).[3] This model of transference is not based on a Freudian theory of conflict but rather of a system maintaining balance, homeostasis, a compensatory model in Jungian terms. Bion, like Jung, made spirituality, religion, and the numinous legitimate phenomena within psychoanalysis, not instead of science but along with it. He followed Jung in his emphasis on pain, being born again, rebirth, myth, and the mystical. Bion, like Jung, offers a critique of Freud's positivism. Bion's "preconceptions" are like Jung's "archetypes," and Bion's "O" is similar to Jung's "Self." Perhaps most importantly for our discussion, Grotstein celebrates that Bion, like Jung before him, emphasized that there is something beyond, before, and in the future—what Bion called *A Memoir of the Future*. For Bion, as for Jung, the unconscious is not only primitive, but it is creative. They both emphasize the visionary, looking forward, the prospective function, working toward the future, and working with the patient's and the analyst's pain.

Here, we see how the dyad unconsciously exchanges injuries, illnesses, as well as angels, demons, and gifts. For Searles (1965), the therapist "introjects the patient's pathogenic conflicts" (p. 214). For Jung and for Searles, the transference means a transfer of the illness itself from client to therapist (Sedgwick, 1993). Grotstein envisions the analysis as a passion play in which the patient projects his demons into the analyst, who sacrifices himself for the patient's sake, thus exorcising the demons (see Harris, Kalb, & Klebanoff, 2016a, 2016b, on ghosts and demons; see Atlas-Koch, 2011, on the *dybbuk*; and see Hoffman, 2011, on Christian influences in psychoanalysis).[4]

We are involved, then, in an unconscious exchange that includes mutual vulnerability (Aron, 2016), suffering and working through past, present, and future, and where the analyst and her body is part of a regulatory system with the patient. This model includes not only the Enigmatic intuitive exchanges mentioned, but also the Pragmatic physical, sensory notions such as tension, affect regulation, and patterns of arousal and overstimulation. What is so often referred to as a "two-person psychology" was first called a "two-body psychology,"[5] and it is crucial to emphasize that it is not only the mind that regulates psychological tensions, but our bodies, ourselves, are essential to the analytic task.

While the immature mind and body are not able to tolerate excessive pain (the baby needs to eat immediately when hungry, her body can't suffer uncomfortable temperatures, and think about how painful it is for a baby to get a vaccine), the parents are the ones who are ideally capable of experiencing, containing, and regulating the baby's pain, so the baby does not collapse. In analysis, as we involve two bodies in that process, it is naïve to think that it is only the analyst who unilaterally regulates the patient's pain. In fact, it is often the opposite, especially because patients are not babies (we sometimes forget that they even have mature sexuality), and they often have the physical capacity to tolerate tension and unconsciously offer their analyst that function. The analyst, again unconsciously, often accepts it. Affect regulation is bi-directional and reciprocal. But as Aron (1996) formulated, the analytic encounter, while mutual in many ways, is not symmetrical; our conscious intention is to help patients develop the ability to tolerate their own suffering, and in our model we ideally do that through living something with our patients, staying alive, tolerating the tension it involves, and through a generative use of our own subjective mind and body.

We are suggesting that the ethos of psychoanalysis be rooted not in neutrality and objectivity, but rather in our acceptance and acknowledgement of mutual vulnerability. In *Precarious Life* (2004), Judith Butler builds on Freud's discussion of mourning to argue that mourning entails an acceptance that one is changed by the loss, that mourning depends on our acceptance of, or submission to, being transformed by the loss, a transformation that we cannot fully control, predict, or determine. The language of the law and legal rights are argued in terms of bounded individuals and groups, delineated subjects before the law. But Butler suggests that while this language establishes our legitimacy within a legal framework, "it does not do justice to passion, grief, and rage, that tear us from ourselves, bind us to others, transport us, undo us, implicate us in lives that are not our own, irreversibly, if not fatally" (p. 25). In other words, we are co-participants, joined on stage, not off the field in the margins, and ethics is grounded in our shared human vulnerability.

For Emmanuel Levinas, the suffering of the face of the other places you in contact with the infinite, the sacred, or the holy. With this view of listening to the suffering stranger (Orange, 2011), the psychoanalytic vocation itself becomes something of a sacred calling. Levinas claims that the Western proclivity to conceive the subject in terms of freedom and rationality mistakenly obscures and distorts our humanity by hiding the significance of human vulnerability and dependence, or what Freud called helplessness. We are calling for a return of the "soul," of the "psyche," of soulfulness and spirit back to psychology.

In *A Meeting of Minds*, Aron (1996) proposed that the essential unifying feature of the relational psychoanalytic tradition, across its range of models, was its highlighting of various aspects of mutuality. These included mutual regulation, mutual recognition, mutual generation of data, mutual transferences, and mutual resistances, among other forms of mutuality, along with an acknowledgement of the necessary asymmetries that were inevitable because of the different roles and responsibilities of patient and analyst. In recent years, Aron (2016) has highlighted the importance of mutual vulnerability. Here, we are adding yet another aspect of mutuality, one that interacts with all the others, namely a specific focus on mutual suffering, a shared and mutually created experience. The very word "patient" derives from the Latin stem of *patiēns*, present participle of *patī*, to undergo, suffer, bear. This is a reminder that we suffer and bear up together, sharing the suffering, and regulate each other's tolerance, bearing of distress. We are co-participants in one regulatory system, playing together one emotional scene. The analyst's holding and containing of shared vulnerability and mutual suffering can take too great a toll on mind, body, and spirit. This aspect of mutuality may even be idealized and turned into a form of masochism. It is precisely for this reason that we so appreciate Adrienne Harris' consistent focus on the need for analysts' self-care (Harris & Sinsheimer, 2008) and Corbett's (2014) call, especially directed at relational analysts because of their emphasis on mutuality, to maintain a private space that allows for contemplation and self-care.

In a classic article in the relational canon, Slavin and Kriegman (1998) suggested that a genuine renegotiation and reintegration of the patient's psyche is far more likely to occur when our patients see what happens when they tap into the fault lines of their therapist's conflicts. When the therapist is able and willing to go where the patient needs them to go, even though it is personally difficult and painful, and when the therapist does this because having a relationship with the patient requires it, that intersubjective experience can be transformative. All the time, our patients provoke us and study the quality of our responsiveness and inner struggle. Our vulnerability and willingness to suffer and change facilitates their sense of trust in exposing their own vulnerability. Perhaps it is obvious that Slavin and Kriegman were influenced by, and in the tradition of, Ferenczi (1932) and Searles (1975) with their emphasis on the patient as therapist to the analyst.

The *Psalms* make use of the symbol of tears to depict human anguish and present God as sharing and helping us regulate and contain our suffering. "Put Thou my tears into Thy bottle; Are they not in Thy book?" (56:8). God holds and contains our tears. In his *Clinical Diary*, Ferenczi (1932) also uses the imagery of tears to depict pooled grief and agony:

> Should it ever occur, as it does occasionally to me, that experiencing another's and my own suffering brings a tear to my eye (and one should not conceal this emotion from the patient), then the tears of doctor and patient mingle in a sublimated

communion, which perhaps finds its analogy only in the mother-child relationship. And this is the healing agent, which like a kind of glue, binds together permanently the intellectually assembled fragments, surrounding even the personality thus repaired with a new aura of vitality and optimism.

(p. 65)

Following Ferenczi's emphasis on mutual vulnerability and his challenge to our overvaluing of words and ideas, and Bion's transformation of Klein's focus on unconscious phantasy into a more fully elaborated intersubjective paradigm, we emphasize the importance of living an experience together, exchanging spirits (in Hebrew, *Ruach*: breath, ghosts) and being interpenetrated. This model of the "dance party" is a dramatic enactment of the unconscious ways in which we live and intermingle with each other, the gathering of sparks, of the souls, of the participants. Those characters and spirits, demons and angels, are all condensations, holograms of the bi-personal field, where we often don't know what belongs to whom. In that meeting of this broadened definition of "mind" (in Hebrew, *Nefesh*, which is also the soul), the meeting is in fact a meeting of mind, body, and spirit. Here, we join Eigen (1981), who in evoking the Bible's words, understands the psychoanalytic venture as requiring all one's heart, soul, and might. We want to highlight that Eigen is dramatizing the need to overcome splitting, to bring together all of one's many selves so that we may participate fully, wholly, and passionately in a "dance party," meeting of minds, bodies, and souls.

Thank you for holding me

We have been discussing ways to bring the soul and spirit back into a dramatic dialogue with the mind and body, a dance party of selves. By now, you might be anticipating that we will end this chapter on the theme of spirituality. Our clinical tale will instead return to sexuality, to the original primal scene of psychoanalysis, the erotic transference. The tale alludes to mutual vulnerability and the erotic dimension of the analytic dyad, which requires mutual regulation of its intensity to remain manageable and productive. Most salient here is the way in which the analyst refrains from interpreting and even purposefully avoids heating up the erotic atmosphere of the analysis, to keep the sexual tensions within useful analytic limits. This illustration is a poignant example of dramatic dialogue that is fueled not by melodramatic action on the analyst's part, but rather by restraint and discipline. Sometimes, it is by what we do not do, as much as what we do, that we co-create with our patients the dramatic dialogue that is at the heart of the story. This tale is a further illustration of the link outlined by Benjamin and Atlas (2015) between the paradigms of attachment theory and the early development of affect regulation, to the realm of sexuality and the too-muchness of excitement. The working through can only happen after the establishment of ongoing regulation. The analytic dyad forms a regulatory system, a lawful third (Benjamin, 2004), from which too-muchness is then modulated and analytically transformed. As this tale describes, in the heat of an erotic transference, suffering is disguised as excitement, hate as longing, and domination masks need. Analyst and patient are together on a stage filled with obstacles.

"Tell me something," my patient Dan asks as he walks into my office on a Monday morning. "What makes you think your work is so different from that of a prostitute?" I recognize his hostile tone but don't rush to interpret this dramatic entrance, as I am pretty familiar, like many other therapists, with the comparison between therapy and prostitution. Many male patients, especially, are preoccupied with paying us, and wonder if we offer love for sale.

"It's emotional prostitution," Dan states, frustrated. He looks at me, waiting for my response, and I know he is anxiously monitoring the impact his words have on me: Am I upset? Did he hurt my feelings or humiliate me? Do I realize that he doesn't believe I can have any real feelings for him, and that I give him something, like a prostitute, only because he pays me?

No one loved Dan. He never had any close friends or a romantic relationship, and in the last few years he has not been in touch with his family. In our first few sessions, he makes sure I know that ever since he was a child, his mother didn't really like him. In fact, she wished he would never have been born. His father committed suicide when Dan's mother was pregnant with him and left Dan, the future baby, alone with a devastated mother, angry and overwhelmed.

"He never loved me either," Dan said. "I'm sure he wanted to get rid of me, and instead, just got rid of himself." Dan feels uninvited into this world and believes that his existence can only cause damage and destruction. Repetition compulsions are everywhere, and in his life, as it often is, reality becomes evidence for internal experience. Reality proves to him, again and again, that he is unlovable and dangerous.

Dan came to see me only about a week after his first analyst of many years died in a car accident. "Aren't you afraid?" He warns me in our first session in his hostile, playful manner. "Maybe if you accept me as a patient, you will die as well. After all, it's clear I kill the people who are supposed to take care of me."

Dan states that he doesn't believe in love. "Loving and being loved is overrated," he says, and I feel how he places me into his scary world, where hate is more tangible than love, where he is bad, and I have no other choice but to soon become bad myself. I am aware that I am set up to reject, betray, and abandon him. Being a patient might put him in touch with the deprived and needy boy that he once was, and that to some degree he still is, and that is too dangerous for him to know. Therefore, Dan constantly reminds me that he buys my services, that it's a business, and that in fact he isn't in any real danger of loving or being loved.

Dan likes the prostitutes he hires. He meets with them when he feels sad and even imagines himself marrying one once in a while, "When she is especially cute and loving." Because he purchases and therefore feels in control, in his mind, prostitutes can never hurt him, and they give him something special. In that sense, referring to me as his prostitute is not only a way to devalue our work, but also an acknowledgement that there is something valuable that he gets in his therapy: crumbs of love. But might it be false love? Dan is worried that in the same way that his girl can fake an orgasm, I can fake one too.

"You would probably never even talk to me if you were not my therapist, if we met elsewhere," he says, never knowing if the women he pays for really enjoy being with him. At the same time, Dan acknowledges that it comforts him to know he pays me. "Then I'm not the needy one," he says.

"At least not the *only* needy one," I answer, and Dan immediately replies, "You are the one who needs me and not the other way around."

Dan is afraid he will be trapped in the position of a needy baby and will no longer be able to function on his own. "In fact," he states, "I'm your boss, and the only thing I will ever give you is money. You can charge me your full fee, but I won't give you anything else. Money, and nothing more." He repeats this to make sure he is clear, and I reassure him that he can buy my services: my time and my genuine investment in the understanding of his mind. "But I can't promise you I will be able to love you," I say. Here, I take the role of his unloving mother, and that makes Dan sad but it's also a relief.

"What do you mean?" Dan opens his blue eyes and asks surprised.

"I mean that I am not sure I will love you. I don't know yet," I say.

"I appreciate that you are telling me the truth," Dan looks straight into my eyes and adds gently, "I want you to know that I really appreciate it." At least on the surface, he prefers that I won't love him at all rather than give him false, tricky love. Hate disguised as love is what he is familiar with. This is the love he got as a child, and that is what he gives to women as an adult. But maybe Dan was surprised not only because I was unloving and noncommittal, but also because this was the first time that it had ever occurred to him that I might ever love him. After all, even in the form of a negation, it was I who introduced the idea of my loving him. He had never directly asked for the promise that I refused. Was this a seduction on my part? Was I hinting to him that love was a possibility if he played his cards right? Is analytic love something that is always held out to the patient in order to motivate their cooperation with the analytic process?

Obviously, this isn't a conversation about love only. It's also about pain, domination, vulnerability, and sex. We, a female therapist and a male patient, are sitting alone in a room, confronting not only our fears of being bad, unloved, and rejected, but also of being seduced, fooled, and betrayed. We revisit the ways in which love and hate intermingle. Through sex, Dan often transforms his hate into false love. He is an experienced lover. He knows how to sexually gratify the random women he goes to bed with, the girls who fall in love with him, and the prostitutes he hires. Hate can be brilliantly transformed into love through passionate lovemaking, and we explore how rage and revenge are always fused with passion and longing.

In 8 years of therapy, we processed Dan's painful and tantalizing childhood. We danced to the rhythm of vulnerability and aggression, examining the delicate balance between love and hate, recognizing how confused they used to be in the house where he grew up. I learned to know Dan and tolerate his attacks on me. I came to like him.

Freud (1906) wrote to Jung that "the [psychoanalytic] Cure is effected by love" (p. 13), and though Freud was referring to the patient's transference love, many analysts have also wondered if it isn't the analyst's love that cures. We believe that as a field, we still struggle with this notion (Bach, 2006; Kuchuck, 2013, in press; Roth, in press; Slavin, 2007).[6] Is therapy about love? Do therapists actually love their patients? Do patients really love their therapists? And if so, how do we ever say goodbye? Who voluntarily ends a loving relationship (Salberg, 2010)? And most important, can love heal our pain?

One evening, on our first session after my summer vacation and during the seventh year of his analysis, Dan walked into the room and said quietly, "I don't know how to start this session. You were away and I had this disturbing dream where I had sex with you." His tone was different than usual. He was soft and careful.

"Do you want to hear the details of my dream?" he asked.

Unlike my usual work with dreams, I do not encourage patients to tell me the details of their erotic dreams and fantasies, simply because I'm aware that it can be, or at least feel like, an enactment of having sex with them. "Sex talk" in therapy—whether via processing a dream or in any other context—is as sexual as any sex talk outside of the analytic room. So how do we actually talk about sex?

Our understanding of the ongoing role of enactment in psychoanalysis has shifted our understanding and technical handling of free association. To encourage the patient to reveal details of sexual thoughts and fantasies is not a neutral act, but is often experienced by patient and analyst as an enactment of sexual seduction.

Historically, analysts, who were predominantly men, insisted that the patient needed to learn the difference between thought and action, to not feel guilty over thoughts, as if they were deeds. They would encourage their, mostly female, patients to tell them their sexual fantasies about the analyst, as if this was just a communication of thoughts with no action taking place (Grand, 2017) As mentioned earlier, from a contemporary point of view, this sharp distinction between speech and action needs deconstruction, as speech does involve a form of action which today we call enactment. Therefore, we are aware that these fantasies can potentially dysregulate a dyad to a point where it will be difficult to maintain an "as if" quality and the symbolic realm of secure play. Here we can see the shift to a frame that includes a delicate monitoring of the dyad's regulation and dysregulation.

In Dan's case, his need for "sex talk" was usually a way to reduce me to the level of a lover (see Freud, 1915b) in order to attack the analysis, to split the sexually desired object from the needed love object on whom one depends. This time, it felt different. I wasn't sure if I was reduced, or maybe elevated to a position that I hadn't yet known.

"I would like to know your thoughts and feelings about having this dream and telling me about it," I said.

Dan moves uncomfortably in his chair; both of us know this kind of investigation usually evoked an attack on me. "Why does it matter how I feel? As if it changes anything to talk about it," he would usually say. This time, he just looks at me and says, "I hear you. Having this dream I realized that I missed you. I was holding you in my arms and that felt good."

I decide to not interpret what I think at the time must have been his only way to feel vulnerable but still in control, understanding that his holding me was also a way of being held by me, while I was away. Something had changed from the times when he needed to perceive me as a dangerous prostitute. Paradoxically, as he was telling me he had sex with me in his dream, I was no longer a devalued sex object that he needed to control. But to arrive here required of both of us that we suspend the power struggle of doer–done-to, one controlling and one controlled, one on top and one on bottom. We each needed to surrender to a larger view of who we were to each other, to accept our vulnerabilities and our fears and to develop a system that regulates rather than one that arouses and dysregulates.

There was a long pause, and then Dan said, "Thank you for not making me feel like a needy little boy, even if I know that I am." His eyes filled with tears and he said gently, "Thank you for holding me."

Notice that everything the patient tells us is not only about what it means, but also about what it does to the system. That "thank you" Dan verbalizes, at other points in the treatment could potentially be "too much," too emotionally dysregulating and arousing. Here, my "silent interpretation" (Ogden, 1979; Spotnitz, 1969), where I tell *myself* that this is Dan's way to feel vulnerable but still in control, can be seen as *my* way of regulating myself using the sexual material as part of a larger understanding of the patient's mind, and creating a dialogue that moved back and forth between the sexual and the non-sexual, arousal and regulation, so to make sure I feel safe, am able to keep my ability to play and be fully present in living through something with my patients. In that sense, being close, loving, and aroused isn't necessarily a progress, or a way to repair childhood wounds, but in fact might repeat childhood deregulation and "too muchness." Again, in the same way love might be a way to disguise hate, arousal can also be a way to avoid intimacy. With its erotic imagery, the dream depicts at-one-ment as Dan holds the analyst, and therefore she also holds him, thus dramatizing the newly emerging achievement of co-suffering through separation.

We do return to tears, moisture, vulnerability. Moisture is associated with femininity, vulnerability, even contamination (Kristeva, 1982). One kind of moisture expresses in displaced form other kinds; moisture leaks, spreads, and flows. Tears as moisture link our minds, bodies, and souls. Excitement and suffering, sex and aggression, the physical and spiritual flow together into a common analytic free associative stream. Interestingly, for Dan, the act of crying was often replaced with the act of masturbation, and tears were replaced with semen. Through displacement, men typically overvalue the hardness of the erection and devalue the moisture of semen, disgusting scum.

This analytic tale isn't a demonstration of the moments when change occurs or of any kind of happy endings—whatever that phrase might conjure. A moment, we believe, is usually a mirror of many implicit previous and future moments, and in Dan's treatment the silent enactment was also a new moment in the analysis, of living through something together.

We never in fact live happily ever after. Perhaps the best we can ask for with our patients, and in life, is to stay alive, to fully live, and to love.

Notes

1 Projective identification (Klein, 1946) was incorporated into post-Freudian theory with Sandler's (1976) notion of role-responsiveness, which in turn has similarities to the post-Jungian idea of the "complementary" countertransference (Jacoby, 1984). It also has similarities to the earlier ego-psychological notion of "the evocation of a proxy" (Wangh, 1962), where another person is used for defensive purposes as an alter ego or proxy and prompted to respond with actions, emotions, judgments, and controls.

2 See especially Aron (2006), Benjamin (2004), Benjamin and Atlas (2015), and Ogden (1994b).

3 Bion was the analyst who more than anyone else besides Jung emphasized the importance of myths—that is, story-telling, drama. Bion, however, according to Grotstein, was not someone who cited his sources and so unfortunately did not credit Jung even though he learned a great deal from him. Bion's work on transformation is like Jung's on transcendence and fits his work on alchemical transformations. Grotstein

argued that Bion's notion of alpha function was a way of talking about the complementarity of conscious and unconscious processing, much like Jung's ideas about compensatory functions of the unconscious.

4 This reminds us of Freud's (1905) comment when he was absorbing Dora's breaking off of her analysis: "No one who, like me, conjures up the most evil of those half-tamed demons that inhabit the human breast, and seeks to wrestle with them, can expect to come through the struggle unscathed" (p. 272).

5 John Rickman, quoted in Balint (1950, p. 123). It was Rickman's paper, influenced directly by Ferenczi, that set both Balint and Winnicott to work on the area of thirdness.

6 Recall our discussion in Chapter 3 of de Forest's (1954) understanding that love was the core ingredient in Ferenczi's understanding of therapeutic action.

Chapter 8

The prequel

This final chapter presents the idea of the prequel to dramatic dialogue. A prequel is a work that forms part of a backstory and so anticipates and hints at what comes later; it engages in a prospective function. We present clinical tales that illustrate how the prequel shapes and colors the treatment narrative. We use the idea of the prequel to highlight the workings of unconscious communication and the intergenerational transmission of trauma and psychodynamics. The book thus ends by dramatizing a constructivist, non-linear conception of time that reworks the field as a temporal as well as spatial metaphor. This chapter enacts the prospective function as well as the conception of time presented throughout the book, showing how afterwardsness (Nachträglichkeit) *reworks the beginning as the prequel anticipates and participates in the emergence of what is subsequent.*

Dramatic dialogues are created unconsciously from the very first contact we have with our patients, or even earlier. We imagine our patients and are invited into their internal world even before we meet. From the brief email or voicemail we receive, from the short conversation we have on the phone, from the way they pronounce their or our name, use the name of the person who referred them, introduce themselves—the drama begins.

A prequel is a literary, dramatic, or filmic work whose story precedes the identified production or "main event" by focusing on proceedings that occur before the central narrative. A prequel is a work that forms part of a backstory and so anticipates and hints at what comes later; it engages in a prospective function. Here are two examples drawn from film and literature. Peter Jackson's film trilogy *The Hobbit* acts as a prequel to *The Lord of the Rings* even though viewers first saw *The Lord of the Rings* a decade earlier. Similarly, *The History of the Holy Grail* (1230) was published two decades after the *Death of Arthur* (1210) but served as its prequel. Like Freud's notion of *Nachträglichkeit*, the prequel challenges our sense of the progressive linearity of time and thus evokes the timelessness of the unconscious. Hence, the reader or viewer absorbs the later story before the chronologically earlier one. In therapy, from the first moment, the patient communicates with us their wishes, fantasies, and conflicts and gives us a role in their drama, the chance to play a character in their narrative. Sometimes only in retrospect, following a later scene, chapter, or dramatization, can we fully understand what happened earlier. Here is an example of a dramatic dialogue: A prequel.

On that Wednesday morning, I was glad to have an unexpected 45 minutes. My 10 a.m. patient was away that week, and as my previous patient left, I opened my computer and started reading the news, wondering if I should eat something before my next patient arrived. I thought about food and started feeling hungry as I heard someone knocking on my door. It was a loud, impatient knock, and I already resented that person who interrupted my break.

I opened the door and looked at the tall guy who was standing there. "Can I help you?" I asked.

"I'm Shawn," he said with a smile. "I think we scheduled to meet at 10 a.m."

He was right. I forgot about him.

Shawn scheduled his first session with me a week earlier. I wrote it in my calendar with my black pen in the Wednesday morning slot. It was clear that I forgot about him.

We began the analytic drama even before we met. Shawn sat for 10 minutes in my waiting room and then knocked on the door.

I opened the session that already began with an apology, and then with a question, "How does it feel to start your analysis with a therapist who didn't open the door?"

"You know, I think you just forgot about me," Shawn said non-chalantly. And before I said anything, he added, smiling, "My first childhood memory is being forgotten on the beach in New Jersey. My mother forgot me there."

"She actually did?" I hear myself asking, realizing that it's not only his mother's act that I question, but my own, as well as the relation between the two.

He continues, "As the story goes, my mother went with my three brothers to a restaurant near the beach, and only as they ordered the food did she realize that I was missing. She panicked; obviously, I was only 4 years old." He smiled again. "She called the police and they found me on the beach after a few hours."

There was nothing dramatic about the way Shawn told me this story. He was calm, forgiving, and even a bit amused by the situation. At least on the surface, I was the one who was concerned about his feelings and about the little boy he was then and now.

"And you, how was it for the little boy that you were to be left alone on the beach and realize that your mother is gone?"

"I don't remember," he answers laconically. "I only know that my biggest fear since then is to be forgotten."

Even before we start, here I am, Shawn's hungry mother who interestingly, like his real mother, thinks about food and forgets about her little boy.

Was that the only time she forgot him? Is that memory lying on other layers of maternal absence? Is this a screen memory? A "tele-scoping" of events (Faimberg, 2005)? Should it be thought of as a model scene (Lachmann & Lichtenberg, 1992)? At that point, I didn't know and could only guess, but I knew that I was there, fully there, an active participant in Shawn's internal drama.

What is the advantage of asking the patient how it feels to begin an analysis with a therapist who doesn't open the door, instead of more directly asking, "How does it feel that I forgot about you?" Here, the therapist is inviting the patient to become a patient. She presents the two characters and opens a symbolic play space where "here I am the therapist and you are the patient." Shawn responds by immediately taking the analyst into his childhood scene as he makes the unconscious link between the forgetting mother and the forgetting analyst. The enactment is generative; it is the prequel to the treatment, and it anticipates and facilitates the emergence of Shawn's childhood experiences, leading him and the analyst, from this point of view, into a territory that they need to explore. Shawn doesn't *tell* the analyst about being forgotten but rather enters the scene as the forgotten child. The analyst is not slowly induced into this countertransference response as we might ordinarily imagine; rather, it is as if she has been solicited or even auditioned to play precisely this character role.

Hence, instead of a rational understanding of the interactions of two individuals or a detailed inquiry into interpersonal reality, we see how "a scene" is developed, or staged, constituted by all the characters in the field to elaborate undigested or unformulated, that is, unconscious states of mind. Rather than making the unconscious conscious, dramatic dialogue (as we mentioned in Chapter 5, like the Bionian perspective on dreaming) attempts to make what is conscious unconscious, to dream the reality, such that it evolves beyond rational understanding. As we discussed in the previous chapter, we view the drama as a dream and the dream as a drama.

As we note, dramas start before they begin, in the same way that a baby is often implanted in her parents' mind before she is actually conceived. Our classic dramas—think Greek tragedies or the Hebrew Bible—are often intergenerational, with the themes and events of one generation continuing and being transformed in the following generation and generations. Earlier generations serve as prequels to the stories of the next, whereas later generations rework and transform the themes of the past, which in turn are given new meaning by these later twists and turns. The rivalry of Cain and Abel at the beginning of Genesis anticipates all the later sibling rivalries to come: Isaac and Ishmael, later Jacob and Esau, and then Joseph and his brothers, and finally Jacob's last blessings of Joseph's children, where once again the younger sibling is put ahead of the elder. And yet, while the earlier story is a prelude to the later, the later story also reworks and gives new meaning to the earlier narrative, a typical expression of Freud's concept of

Nachträglichkeit, a supplementary afterwardsness or retroactive reworking (see Laplanche & Pontalis, 1973).[1] Drama never starts at the beginning of the story, for the beginning always has a prequel. Stories never end, but neither do they ever begin at the beginning. Here again, we suggest a nonlinear perspective on time. As Freud (1915a) wrote,

> The processes of the system Ucs are timeless—i.e., they are not ordered temporally, are not altered by the passage of time; they have no reference to time at all. Reference to time is bound up, once again, with the work of the system Cs.
>
> (p. 187)

Our reference to conception and childbirth is a loaded metaphor, so to speak. We have in mind of course the intergenerational transmission of trauma and the passing on of themes and conflicts from one generation to the next, and we also have in mind so-called "primitive" unconscious communication between mother and infant, and later between analyst and patient, container and contained. But we are also hinting at Bion's (1977) caesura, a link between mature thought and feeling and intra-uterine life. Bion's caesura serves as a model for spanning what seems like unbridgeable states of mind. Where is the caesura, the link and break, the moment of pause between not yet knowing our patient and being in an analytic relationship with them? What is the caesura between our being two individuals, strangers, and being an analytic dyad? What is that caesura that gives birth to the analytic third? How did the patient communicate with the analyst, in whatever remarkably subtle form, his unconscious phantasy, wish, and terror of being forgotten? What were the subtle behaviors that might have "induced" or "nudged" the analyst to become "role-responsive" or to respond with such a precise "complementary countertransference"?

Certainly, we are not the first psychoanalysts to appreciate the power of unconscious communication. Curiosity and interest in unconscious communication certainly goes back to the early history of psychoanalysis, among Freud, Jung, and Ferenczi especially, and of course this has a prehistory, a prequel, in even earlier formulations, in spiritism and religion, while it also serves as a precursor to later developments, such as by Bion, Grotstein, Eigen, Bass, and Suchet, among others. Some analysts have focused on Pragmatic explanations—that is, an interest in the subtle behaviors by which a patient communicates or induces responses in the analyst. Other analysts and theorists are less interested in the behaviors or actions and adopt a more Enigmatic attitude, and some, like Laplanche, make use of both: for example, his Enigmatic Message includes the mystery of unconscious intergenerational transmission, while his stress on the mother's handling and holding of the infant points to more Pragmatic formulations.

The Enigmatic emphasizes that unconscious communication is the way the mind works; at some deep level, we are all interconnected, our minds part of a larger system, where one part of a system always effects and communicates with other sub-systems. Unconscious communication is simply an expression of minds being inherently intersubjective. Intersubjectivity is not a joining of separate subjects but rather precedes and is the ground for it. On a deep unconscious level, we are always already interconnected and at one. Our separateness and boundedness is a conscious, adult, rational overlay, as we discussed in Chapter 7.

In our emphasis on unconscious communication and the generative use of the analyst's subjectivity, we are not only calling for something more than interpretation, as we have seen both Ferro and Searles emphasize in earlier chapters. In displacing interpretation with dramatic dialogue and generative enactment, we are suggesting that the analyst searches to become at one with the psychic reality of the present moment, and thus consciousness is displaced by the unconscious, awareness by intuition, insight by experience.

Jung dreaming his patient

Consider the following clinical tale and its embedded prequel, told by Carl Jung (1961), which we think elegantly brings many of these themes together.[2] Jung recalls a case of a Jewish woman who came to see him for an initial consultation. He surprises the reader by stating that the case began with a dream that he had the night prior to meeting his new patient. In Jung's dream, a young girl who he did not recognize came to him as a patient. While she was telling him about herself, Jung had the thought, still in the dream, that he did not understand her at all. But he suddenly had the idea that she must have an unusual father complex.

On the following day, Jung had scheduled a consultation at 4 p.m.[3] A young, pretty, smart, and wealthy Jewish woman appeared, suffering for some years from anxiety. She had already been in an analysis, which was interrupted because her analyst told her that if he continued to treat her, it would result in the destruction of his marriage. Note that Jung gives us only sketchy information about the woman's background. We do not know any of the details of what went wrong in the previous treatment or what led to this derailment. We also do not know whether Jung himself had scheduled the appointment for the consultation. Had he spoken with her prior to the meeting, or had his secretary set up the consultation?

Jung took an anamnesis, but could not discover any satisfactory explanation. She was, despite her neurosis, a well-adapted, enlightened secular thinker. Suddenly, while listening to her, he recalled his dream from the night before and immediately believed that she was "the little girl" of his dream. Jung then tells us a fascinating aspect of his technique. When he cannot formulate the dynamics of a case based on taking a history of the patient and their immediate family, he then asks the patient about the previous generation, the grandparents. When he mentions her grandfather, the patient closed her eyes in deep thought, and Jung said that he knew that he had hit upon "the key to the case." It turned out that her grandfather was a rabbi, and as Jung quickly infers, he was a Chasidic *tsaddik* or holy saint who the patient described as possessing "second sight" or clairvoyance. But of course, she insists, she did not believe in such mystical nonsense.

Jung now believed that he had enough data to formulate the dynamics of the case and the etiology of her neurosis. He explained to the young woman assuredly that her grandfather was a holy man, but that her father had rebelled and become an apostate to the faith. Her father had betrayed Judaism and turned his back on God, and therefore at least implicitly on his own father. Jung told her that she had become neurotic because the "fear of God" had gotten into her, and this explanation struck the young woman like a bolt of lightning. One can see this as an example of how Jung's therapeutic goal was for the patient to achieve individuation, and for Jung, God and the Self are one, so that to find and elaborate one's Self is equivalent to finding God in oneself. One might say that for Jung, individuating, being born again, and finding God are equivalent goals of treatment.

There is more to this story, including Jung's reporting further dreams that he believed confirm and expand his narrative. We see how Jung understood this woman's neurosis to be the result of intergenerational transmission, not just an intrapsychic conflict, but also an intergenerational one. The unresolved conflict between her grandfather and her father over religion plagued her. It is as if she embodied their ghosts and lived out, embodied, their intergenerational battle (see Harris, Kalb, & Klebanoff, 2016a). The fight between her forebears anticipated and served as a prequel to her own internal conflict and neurosis. She had consciously sided with her father, but had dissociated, as irrational nonsense, her religious, spiritually inclined self, the Goddess within herself. By exposing the numinous within her, by bringing to light her "fear of God"—that is to say, by building a bridge to her dissociated spiritual self—Jung cured her and her symptoms reportedly disappeared.

We will now speak in our own voices, rather than in Jung's, stepping away from his absorption in the story to look at what he was doing clinically from our perspective. We extrapolate from the limited data provided by Jung to illustrate how the notion of dramatic dialogue helps us conceptualize why and how Jung's approach may have led him to what he was convinced was a dramatic success.

On the manifest level, Jung's thesis is simply that this young woman had become alienated from her spiritual side, the Goddess within her. She had become one-sidedly secular and rational and thus left no space for spirituality or faith. He believed that he confronted her with her dissociation and hence enabled her cure by facilitating "individuation," the reclamation of split-off parts of herself.

What we are elaborating is the unarticulated or unformulated intersubjective and interpersonal context in which central dynamics are enacted, suggesting that a variety of characters are brought onto the analytic stage, leading to transformation of the field. Jung in his very certainty asserts his proclamations that sound omnipotent; he knows that she is "the little girl" he dreamed of the night before. Not that he associated to her or suspects a connection, but he knows. He is the mystic and prophet who dreams up his patient even before meeting her. He becomes the grandfather, *in vivo*, the *tsaddik* who is known to have "second sight." He asks just the right questions and proclaims her undeniable cure. And so, while he is interpreting to her that she has dissociated the Goddess within her, he enacts being the mystic saintly grandfather or even that very God whom she now may worship; after all, she has gone from being a young woman to being his little girl.

What we see, whether deliberate or not, is that Jung facilitates a process in which both sides of a split are brought onto the analytic stage and enacted or played out between them with the usual reversals and inversions. Jung enacted with the patient—that is to say, he dramatized with her—several of the split-off roles that were in active contention in her psychic life. He and she together played out the roles of grandfather and father, grandfather and God, father and God, daughter and father. They did not just talk about her belief in God or lack of belief, nor did they just talk about her grandfather's and father's conflict. Rather, these roles were brought into the theater of the analysis through a dramatic dialogue that heightened its intensity and made it affectively alive, even if now neither of them were self-conscious or explicitly aware of what it was they were enacting. In this regard, Jung's trust in himself, while it might be a liability in other respects, served him well in facilitating his trust in his own unconscious intuitive processes, allowing him to enter his patient's world with much immediacy and intensity. In enacting this drama, Jung became the incarnation of "the little girl's" grandfather, the religious saint. She could now, through this dramatic dialogue with Jung in the role of her righteous grandfather, rework her inner conflicts, and in so doing repair the damage that began in previous generations. The prequel might refer to Jung's dream, dreamt before he met this patient, and it also may refer to the conflicts of the previous generations that anticipate the patient's current conflicts.

Jung, acting Godlike at one moment, may keep her in the role of little subservient girl, whereas at another moment he may allow for her identification with a Godlike figure. By understanding her dissociation in the context of intergenerational conflict, Jung may have allowed her to move past the impasse of her conflicting loyalties. But these interpretations or understandings might be powerless without the generative enactment implied in Jung himself acting the part of the wise old man, saint and clairvoyant, who also appreciated and celebrates his patient as Goddess.[4] Even as she was describing her grandfather's clairvoyance as nonsense, Jung himself was making use of a prophetic dreaming up of the patient—that is, making clinical use of what we are calling a prequel to dramatic dialogue.

Roy's tale presents another way of thinking about splitting and the unconscious role of the analyst in the dramatic prequel.

Lovers and splitting

When I heard Roy's voice message, I was on the street, walking back home from the office. It was 9 p.m., and I listened to the messages on my cell phone. There was something in his tone that made me like him.

I can't recall the details of our initial phone conversation the next morning, maybe because the only thing I was left with was a strong feeling. Strangely, I was very curious about this guy. I liked him more than I usually like new patients after talking with them for only 3 minutes. Even then, I wondered what it was that I was being solicited to play. Sometimes a person knows things without knowing that they know, an Enigmatic Knowing (Atlas, 2015). I knew that I felt drawn to Roy in a way that was not typical, I knew that, and knew that I knew it, but couldn't yet know more.

I tried to reflect on my feelings: What was it about him that I found likable? He was respectful, polite, and in fact I was almost sure he had a smile on his face when he spoke with me. Mostly, it seems like he was looking forward to his meeting with me, or was it me who was looking forward to meeting him? What role was I playing? Who were we to each other? Who were we avoiding being?

While we propose that in every initial conversation the analyst already plays some role in the patient's internal drama, only in retrospect do I realize that in that interaction I was already a developed character in Roy's internal world. I couldn't have known this then, even if I had thought it. I couldn't have thought it, even if I had known it.

In the first session, I learned that Roy was married with three children, and in the following session, when I asked how he felt about our first session, he told me that he thinks he fell in love with me and would like me to be his lover. I hear this wish, almost always, in line with what Freud (1915b) describes as the function of resistance in transference-love. Falling in love with your therapist, as mentioned in Chapter 7, to some degree or another, is always an unconscious resistance to change and to the analytic work. It is a wish to transform the analysis into a love affair and the analyst to a lover and thereby to avoid pain and resist change. I wondered about that out loud with Roy. "Maybe," I suggested, "it's easier to have a love affair than to be in analysis."

"Maybe I'm more used to that," he joked. "If you become my lover, you will solve all my problems and I won't need an analyst."

"And what if I'm your analyst?" I asked seriously.

"Then I will have to look at my problems," he said. "Then, I'm in trouble." He looked at me and then asked in a semi-naïve way, "But hey, can't you be both?"

One might feel irritated or even shocked at his directness, or feel flattered for being so eagerly seduced, or one might acknowledge being challenged, provoked, or probed.

Freud (1915b) warns us that

> He [The analyst] must recognize that the patient's falling in love is induced by the analytic situation and is not to be attributed to the charms of his own person; so that he has no grounds whatever for being proud of such a "conquest", as it would be called outside analysis.
>
> (p. 161)

As you can gather, from the very first contact the drama had begun, potentially intense and hot, but in some ways clearly a way to create an erotic environment and disrupt our ability to think as an analytic couple and to maintain the symbolic realm. I was pulled into that dynamic from the first time I heard Roy's voice, even before I spoke with him, and in those first sessions our focus was mainly on the unconscious purpose that an affair might serve, and the ambivalence about being engaged in a therapy as in any intimate relationship. An affair, in that sense, is also a way to make sure he isn't fully known, controlled, and owned by the other. Each woman then gets only a little piece of him, and the rest remains hidden.

Three months into the analysis, Roy started an extramarital affair with a woman who was a therapist. There is much to say about this choice and about his analysis, which lasted six years. Mostly, I believe, we understood how his affairs helped him to be the aggressive, angry boy that he couldn't be with his mother and then with his wife. We questioned if now, when the other therapist is his lover, it is she who gets to know the parts of him that he will come to hide from me. With his lover, he could have wild sex, he could be the bad boy, while with the other women in his life—his mother, his wife, and now me—he is always the nice little boy who protects us from his anger and hate.

Roy was intensely conflicted, both wanting to be known and wanting to remain unknown, wanting to be seen and wanting to stay hidden. In trying to seduce his analyst and make her a lover, he expressed what is typically thought of as "resistance," specifically, defending against being exposed as needy and greedy, as well as angry and destructive out of resentment of his unfulfilled longings. Being transformed into his lover, his analyst would not be able to analyze him and would not see these destructive qualities. At the same time, he imagined that as his lover, his analyst would love him and gratify all his needs, even accepting his greedy, sexually exploitative, and aggressive dark side. By turning his therapist into a lover, Roy would destroy his treatment, punishing himself by depriving himself of the therapy he needed. This would be a way to avoid the

feelings of guilt that would emerge. For as much as he sought gratification, he did not feel entitled to authentic fulfillment.

Roy's split self and object world was enacted unconsciously from
the first voicemail he left his future analyst, and she responded to it
by immediately having feelings towards him. She was playing the
lover even before she actually met Roy, and only by realizing her role
in his internal drama could they work through the internal split and
strive for integration, where he could be a little boy with active fantasies of breastfeeding as well as an independent sexual master. His
unconscious wish for growth and integration was there from the first
session, when Roy seductively suggested, "Hey, can't you be both?"

We want to make the distinction between "can't you be both?" as
an omnipotent phantasy—that is, a manic defense—in contrast to
what we come to later, where the question represents an acceptance
of the depressive position, meaning that you no longer need to maintain the split. In other words, his initial statement "hey, can't you be
both?" reflects his wanting to have it all—the therapist should be both
mother and whore, wife and girlfriend, analyst and lover. While this
may look like integration, since he wants the therapist to be both, it is
in fact being used defensively to avoid the recognition that he can't
have it all. Similarly, for the therapist, it could embody the omnipotent
phantasy that she could give him everything, thus for both patient and
analyst the phantasy that she could be both analyst and lover negates
the acceptance of limits symbolized in the depressive position.

Splitting, while often thought of as a "primitive" defense or developmental deficit, also serves development and growth by preserving
contradictory affects and relations until they can be integrated and
owned. So-called "primitivity," with its stereotypically racist implications, may then be seen not only as a deficit and handicap, but
also may be understood affirmatively as having a prospective function. Indeed, Klein (1946) views splitting as an *achievement* of the
paranoid-schizoid position. We should not view it only as a deficit,
but also as an accomplishment.

To maintain his split selves and objects (multiple self-states),
Roy made use of a variety of people to play various roles and

characters in his drama. Splitting was maintained and enacted in a complex network of interactions and particularly in triangles, where a relationship with one person balanced and so preserved his relationship to another. He could maintain his relationship with his wife by having a secret affair, maintain his relationship with me by falling in love with another therapist who was like me in many respects, and preserve his relationship with her by expressing his aggression in his marriage and therapy. It was not enough to understand these dynamics, but rather to recognize that they are always already being played out and do not only exist within an enclosed or isolated mind. They are enacted and maintained intersubjectively, and it is precisely because they are enacted with the therapist that they can be experimented with and gradually modified. As one role develops, shifts, evolves, so will the whole system of relationships, the interpersonal field, for a change in one part of the field inevitably affects the entire field.

Dramatic dialogue as a model of therapeutic action is rooted in the understanding that what allows for change in therapy is precisely the recognition that our dynamics are always played out, enacted, dramatized with the analyst on an analytic stage where, as Bleger (1969/2012) observed, nothing ever has only one meaning, and "our psychoanalytic theory is basically dynamic, whereas the theory implicit in our practice is basically dramatic" (p. 994). The dramatic point of view, in contrast to the traditional dynamic point of view, with its use of mechanical forces, adopts a humanistic outlook with a focus on human life and behavior, as it is lived between people.

"All you need is love"

Before turning to our last tale—as a prequel to it, so to speak—let's return to our earlier discussion of *Nachträglichkeit* and supplement it. In Freud's reconstruction of the Wolfman's primal scene, told in his 1918 account, "From the History of an Infantile Neurosis," we derive his clinical understanding of *Nachträglichkeit*, a nonlinear view of time. What comes later in the story, the main event, supplements the meaning of what came earlier, the prequel. It was just before his fourth birthday that the patient had his famous dream of threatening white wolves, the dream that inaugurated his childhood phobias, as he recalls some 20 years later in his analysis. Freud reconstructs the primal scene of age one and a half, in which he watched his parents in bed, but it is never actually remembered by the patient. Freud suggests it might well have been a condensation of his parents and observing the copulation of dogs. At age one and a half, when it supposedly took place or was fantasized, the young boy did not experience the primal scene as a trauma. It only became a trauma at age four, when the dream reactivated the scene, but this time with sexual and frightening meanings. It now had sexual significance because in the interim, between the primal scene and the dream, the boy had been seduced by his sister, his nannie had threatened him with castration for masturbating, and he was now at the height of Oedipal excitations with sexual wishes directed toward his father. Thus, Freud makes clear, the boy's fear of castration did not exist at the time of the primal scene but was only supplemented by that anxiety retroactively, at age four, when he imagined that being penetrated by his father would necessitate that he be castrated as he imagined his mother was.

Remember too, that all of this account was Freud's construction some 20 years after these supposed childhood events, and Freud acknowledged that his reconstruction was based on a chain of inferences. We may therefore ask: When did the Wolfman's primal scene take place? When did it become associated with castration anxiety? Was it at one and a half, at four, or in his twenties, when it was constructed by Freud, or co-constructed with Freud? Is the primal scene the prequel in this narrative, or is the analytic scene the prequel to the primal scene? Which event initiated the sequence? What is most significant about this primal Freudian story, never mind the Oedipal content or childhood sexuality, is the way Freud's narrative treats time as fluid and dynamic, always being reworked, re-transcribed, and not as a fixed linear progression. The narrative never actually has a beginning, and it never in fact ends.

As you read the next clinical tale, keep in mind the sense of time and sequence evoked by the story, and you will see that the notion of a prequel is an attempt to dislodge our usual sense of time's linearity. Follow along as the analyst anticipates her patient in the prequel to the session, but as you listen to the session, consider that what happens later may supplement the prequel and give it newer meanings. Might you read this clinical tale, and reorder its narrative sequence, so that what is highlighted as the main story and what appears to be the prequel may shift over time?

Also, yet another prequel, we introduced the story by referring to Freud's construction of the primal scene. The primal scene evokes the Oedipal predicament of the child's not knowing with whom to identify. Does the boy, for example, identify with the mother or with the father? Is he identified with an actor inside the scene or as an outside observer to a dyad from which he is excluded? The primal scene may be viewed as a paradigm of multiple self and object relations, of multiple self-states interacting with personifications of others, a "dance party." As you read the following story, look for triangles, multiple identifications, and shifts in perspective, or multiple vertices, to use Bion's (1965) idiom.

This last tale starts with a soundtrack. The analyst is sitting in her chair, waiting for her patient Leah, who scheduled a double session for that morning. The analyst is humming to herself, "*All we need is love.*"

The patient is late. She already missed the first part of the session and is now 15 minutes late for the second part. "This was predictable," the analyst thought to herself. "Well, maybe I'll open my computer and prepare for next week, while waiting."

It is a few days before the Christmas break, and the analyst was planning to take a week off and, with her partner, finish the book that they were writing. That thought made her happy, and she imagined an isolated island, with just the two of them on it, co-creating an imaginary world that belongs to only them.

The song in her head kept playing, and she starts feeling irritated that she isn't able to shut it off and recognizes that she is singing incorrect lyrics. She wondered whether she was singing that song to herself, or maybe to the patient she was waiting for. Is she expressing her own feelings about the week of writing with her partner, or maybe it's preparation for her patient's arrival? "Do Leah and I even love each other?" she asked herself, and thought about Leah's capacity to love and her anxiety about committing to one partner.

There was an impatient knock on the door. Leah stormed in, apologizing. "I overslept," in a voice that sounded too loud, as she sat on the couch. "Mornings are always hard," she added and then said, "I thought about it on my way, that I'm so glad I'm not going away on a vacation this year. Do you remember last year, when I was with Sam and we took a week vacation to the Caribbean—what a nightmare that was?" She looked at the analyst for the first time and then added, "It was only me and him for a long time on that island and time seemed endless."

"You don't want to be alone on an island with someone," the analyst noted, and Leah immediately responded, "Not with one person, no. I get bored."

"It's too long and too close."

"Exactly."

"Maybe you are also telling me something here about this morning; isn't a double session similar to being on an isolated island with one person, for too long and too close?"

"NO!" Leah shouted, "I just couldn't wake up in the morning, that's all. Don't read into it."

The analyst was silent. She realized her interpretation came too quickly and that it was too intimate to talk about her and Leah as an analytic couple. After all, Leah was telling her about how anxious she becomes when the situation is dyadic. But then right away, Leah brought more people into the room: "It's only because I was at a party too late last night, with tons of people. It was amazing. And I told all of my friends, let's make a toast for the New Year. We raised our glasses in the air and I exclaimed, '*All we need is love*.'"

Notes

1 For those of us who spent years studying the Hebrew Bible in the Talmudic tradition, this sense of nonlinear time is familiar, as the rabbis continually emphasized that "there is no before or after in the Torah" [*en mukdam u-me'uhar ba-Torah*]. Chronology was always shifting and unsettled; time is malleable.

2 We refer the reader to Jung's text for all of the fascinating details, as we can only summarize highlights here.

3 Jung does not say why he mentions the time, but we should recall that the number four had meaning and significance to Jung, representing the wholeness of the self and individuation.

4 In a later dream, in fact, Jung pictures himself on his knees worshipping his patient as Goddess.

References

Aguayo, J., & Malin, B. (2013). *Wilfred Bion: Los Angeles seminars and supervision*. London: Karnac.

Akhtar, S. (2007). Four roadblocks in approaching Masud Khan. *Psychoanalytic Quarterly, 76*, 991–995.

Arlow, J. A. (1986). Psychoanalysis and time. *Journal of the American Psychoanalytic Association, 34*, 507–528.

Aron, L. (1991). Working through the past—Working toward the future. *Contemporary Psychoanalysis, 27*, 81–109.

Aron, L. (1995). The internalized primal scene. *Psychoanalytic Dialogues, 5*, 195–237.

Aron, L. (1996). *A meeting of minds: Mutuality in psychoanalysis*. Hillsdale, NJ: The Analytic Press.

Aron, L. (2000). Self-reflexivity and the therapeutic action of psychoanalysis. *Psychoanalytic Psychology, 17*, 667–689.

Aron, L. (2003a). Clinical outbursts and theoretical breakthroughs: A unifying theme in the work of Stephen A. Mitchell. *Psychoanalytic Dialogues, 13*, 259–273.

Aron, L. (2003b). The paradoxical place of enactment in psychoanalysis: Introduction. *Psychoanalytic Dialogues, 13*, 623–631.

Aron, L. (2006). Analytic impasse and the third: Clinical implications of intersubjectivity theory. *International Journal of Psychoanalysis, 87*, 350–368.

Aron, L. (2014). "With you I'm born again": Themes and fantasies of birth and the family circumstances surrounding birth as these are mutually evoked in patient and analyst. *Psychoanalytic Dialogues, 24*, 341–357.

Aron, L. (2016). Mutual vulnerability: An ethic of clinical practice. In D. Goodman (Ed.), *The ethical turn: Otherness and subjectivity in contemporary psychoanalysis* (pp. 19–41). London: Routledge.

Aron, L., & Atlas, G. (2015). Generative enactment: Memories from the future. *Psychoanalytic Dialogues, 25*, 309–324.

Aron, L., & Bushra, A. (1998). Mutual regression: Altered states in the psychoanalytic situation. *Journal of the American Psychoanalytic Association, 46*, 389–412.

Aron, L., & Harris, A. (Eds.) (1993). *The legacy of Sándor Ferenczi.* Hillsdale, NJ: The Analytic Press.

Aron, L., & Lieberman, A. (2017). In memory of Harold Searles: 1918–2015. *Psychoanalytic Dialogues, 27*, 182–191.

Aron, L., & Starr, K. (2013). *A psychotherapy for the people: Toward a progressive psychoanalysis.* New York, NY: Routledge.

Atlas, G. (2013a). Eat, pray, dream: Contemporary use of dreams in psychoanalysis. *Contemporary Psychoanalysis, 49*, 239–246.

Atlas, G. (2013b). Eating, cooking and the space between: Response to panelists' commentaries. *Contemporary Psychoanalysis, 49*, 276–286.

Atlas, G. (2015). Touch me, know me: The enigma of erotic longing. *Psychoanalytic Psychology, 32*, 123–139.

Atlas, G. (2016). *The enigma of desire: Sex, longing and belonging in psychoanalysis.* London: Routledge.

Atlas-Koch, G. (2011). The bad father, the sinful son, and the wild ghost: A psychoanalytic exploration of the *Dybbuk. Psychoanalytic Perspectives, 8*, 238–251.

Bach, S. (1998). Two ways of being. *Psychoanalytic Dialogues, 8*, 657–673.

Bach, S. (2006). *Getting from here to there: Analytic love, analytic process.* Hillsdale, NJ: The Analytic Press.

Bach. S. (2016). *Chimeras and other writings.* Astoria, NY: International Psychoanalytic Books.

Balint, M. (1950). *The basic fault: Therapeutic aspects of regression.* Evanston, IL: Northwestern University Press.

Baranger, M., & Baranger, W. (2008). The analytic situation as a dynamic field. *International Journal of Psychoanalysis, 89*, 795–826.

Bass, A. (2015). The dialogue of unconsciouses: Mutual analysis and the uses of the self in contemporary relational psychoanalysis. *Psychoanalytic Dialogues, 25*, 2–17.

Beebe, B., & Lachmann, F. M. (2002). *Infant research and adult treatment: Co-constructing interactions.* Hillsdale, NJ: The Analytic Press.

Benjamin, J. (1998). *Like subjects, love objects: Essays on recognition and sexual difference.* New Haven, CT: Yale University Press.

Benjamin, J. (2004). Beyond doer and done-to: An intersubjective view of thirdness. *Psychoanalytic Quarterly, 73*, 5–46.

Benjamin, J. (2009). A relational psychoanalysis perspective on the necessity of acknowledging failure in order to restore the facilitating and containing features of the intersubjective relationship (the shared third). *International Journal of Psychoanalysis, 90*, 441–450.

Benjamin, J. (2010). Where's the gap and what's the difference? *Contemporary Psychoanalysis, 46*, 112–119.

Benjamin, J. (2013). Thinking together, differently: Thoughts on Bromberg and intersubjectivity. *Contemporary Psychoanalysis, 49*, 356–379.

Benjamin, J. (2015). Response to Aron and Atlas: Cooking up a storm—together. *Psychoanalytic Dialogues, 25*, 335–343.

Benjamin, J. (2018). *Beyond doer and done to.* London and New York: Routledge.

Benjamin, J., & Atlas, G. (2015). The "too muchness" of excitement: Sexuality in light of excess, attachment and affect regulation. *International Journal of Psychoanalysis, 96*, 39–63.

Bion, W. R. (1959). Attacks on linking. *International Journal of Psychoanalysis, 40*, 308–315.

Bion, W. R. (1962a). *Learning from experience.* London: Heinemann.

Bion, W. R. (1962b). The psycho-analytic study of thinking. *International Journal of Psychoanalysis, 43*, 306–310.

Bion, W. R. (1965). *Transformations.* London: Tavistock.

Bion, W. R. (1967). Notes on memory and desire. In J. Aguayo & B. Malin (Eds.), *Wilfred Bion: Los Angeles seminars and supervision* (pp. 136–138). London: Karnac.

Bion, W. R. (1970). *Attention and interpretation.* London: Tavistock.

Bion, W. R. (1977). *Two papers: The grid and caesura.* London, Karnac, 1989.

Bion, W. R. (1991). *A memoir of the future*: Books 1–3. London: Karnac.

Bleger, J. (1969/2012). Theory and practice in psychoanalysis: Psychoanalytic praxis. *International Journal of Psychoanalysis, 93*, 993–1003.

Bollas, C. (1989). *Forces of destiny: Psychoanalysis and human idiom.* London: Free Association Books.

Bollas, C. (1992). *Being a character: Psychoanalysis and self experience.* London: Routledge.

Boston Change Process Study Group. (2013). Enactment and the emergence of new relational organization. *Journal of the American Psychoanalytic Association, 61,* 727–749.

Brennan, B. W. (2009). Ferenczi's forgotten messenger: The life and work of Izette de Forest. *American Imago, 66*(4), 427–455.

Breuer, J. (1893). Fräulein Anna O.: Case histories from *Studies on hysteria.* In J. Strachey (Ed. & Trans.), *The standard edition of the complete psychological works of Sigmund Freud* (Vol. 2, pp. 19–47). London: Hogarth Press.

Bromberg, P. M. (1994). "Speak! That I may see you": Some reflections on dissociation, reality, and psychoanalytic listening. *Psychoanalytic Dialogues, 4,* 517–547.

Bromberg, P. M. (1998a). *Standing in the spaces: Essays on clinical process, trauma, and dissociation.* Hillsdale, NJ: The Analytic Press.

Bromberg, P. M. (1998b). Staying the same while changing: Reflections on clinical judgment. *Psychoanalytic Dialogues, 8,* 225–236.

Bromberg, P. M. (2006). *Awakening the dreamer: Clinical journeys.* Mahwah, NJ: The Analytic Press.

Brown, L. J. (2011). *Intersubjective processes and the unconscious: An integration of Freudian, Kleinian and Bionian perspectives.* London: Routledge.

Butler, J. (2004). *Precarious life: The powers of mourning and violence.* London: Verso.

Caston, J. (2011). Agency as a psychoanalytic idea. *Journal of the American Psychoanalytic Association, 59,* 907–938.

Civitarese, G. (2005). Fire at the theatre: (Un)reality of/in the transference. *International Journal of Psychoanalysis, 86,* 1299–1316.

Civitarese, G. (2013). *The violence of emotions: Bion and post–Bionian psychoanalysis.* Routledge: London.

Civitarese, G., & Ferro, A. (2013). The meaning and use of metaphor in analytic field theory. *Psychoanalytic Inquiry, 33,* 190–209.

Cooper, S. H. (2000). *Objects of hope: Exploring possibility and limit in psychoanalysis.* Hillsdale, NJ: The Analytic Press.

Corbett, K. (2014). The analyst's private space: Spontaneity, ritual, psychotherapeutic action, and self-care. *Psychoanalytic Dialogues, 24*, 637–647.

Culbert-Koehn, J. (1997). Between Bion and Jung: A talk with James Grotstein. *The San Francisco Jung Institute Library Journal, 15*, 15–32.

Davies, J. M. (1996). Linking the "pre-analytic" with the postclassical: Integration, dissociation, and the multiplicity of unconscious process. *Contemporary Psychoanalysis, 32*, 553–576.

Davies, J. M. (2003). Reflections on Oedipus, post–Oedipus, and termination: Commentary on paper by Steven Cooper. *Psychoanalytic Dialogues, 13*, 65–75.

Davies, J. M. (2004). Whose bad objects are we anyway? Repetition and our elusive love affair with evil. *Psychoanalytic Dialogues, 14*(6), 711–732.

Davies, J. M. (2016). To dream, perchance to think: Discussion of papers by Noelle Burton and Christopher Bonovitz. *Psychoanalytic Dialogues, 26*, 322–330.

Davies, J. M., & Frawley, M. G. (1994). *Treating adult survivors of childhood sexual abuse.* New York, NY: Basic Books.

De Forest, I. (1942). The therapeutic technique of Sándor Ferenczi. *International Journal of Psychoanalysis, 23*, 120–139.

De Forest, I. (1954). *The leaven of love: A development of the psychoanalytic theory and technique of Sándor Ferenczi.* New York, NY: Harper Brothers.

Deleuze, G., & Guattari, F. (1987). *A thousand plateaus: Capitalism and schizophrenia* (B. Massumi, Trans.). Minneapolis, MN: University of Minnesota Press.

Eagle, M. (1993). Enactments, transference, and symptomatic cure: A case history. *Psychoanalytic Dialogues, 3*, 93–110.

Eigen, M. (1981). The area of faith in Winnicott, Lacan and Bion. *International Journal of Psychoanalysis, 62*, 413–433.

Ekstein, R., & Wallerstein, J. (1956). Observations on the psychotherapy of borderline and psychotic children. *Psychoanalytic Study of the Child, 11*, 303–311.

Emuna, R. (1994). *Acting for real: Drama therapy process, technique, and performance.* London: Routledge.

Erikson, E. H. (1946). Ego development and historical change: Clinical notes. *Psychoanalytic Study of the Child, 2*, 359–396.

Faimberg, H. (2005). *The telescoping of generations: Listening to the narcissistic links between generations.* London: Routledge.

Faimberg, H. (2013). The "as-yet situation" in Winnicott's "Fragment of an analysis": Your father "never did you the honor of" . . . yet. *Psychoanalytic Quarterly, 82,* 849–875.

Farber, D. (2014). A memoir of the future of contemporary psychoanalysis: The gentle *jouissance* of Giuseppe Civitarese. *Fort Da, 20,* 33–55.

Feldman, M. (1997). Projective identification: The analyst's involvement. *International Journal of Psychoanalysis, 78,* 227–241

Ferenczi, S. (1931). Child-analysis in the analysis of adults. *International Journal of Psychoanalysis, 12,* 468–482.

Ferenczi, S. (1932). *The clinical diary of Sándor Ferenczi* (J. Dupont, Ed., M. Balint & N. Z. Jackson, Trans.). Cambridge, MA: Harvard University Press, 1988.

Ferro, A. (2006). Clinical implications of Bion's thought. *International Journal of Psychoanalysis, 87,* 989–1003.

Ferro, A. (2009). Transformations in dreaming and characters in the psychoanalytic field. *International Journal of Psychoanalysis, 90,* 209–230.

Ferro, A., & Civitarese, G. (2015). *The analytic field and its transformations.* London, Routledge.

Ferro, A., & Nicoli, L. (2017). *The new analyst's guide to the galaxy.* London: Karnac.

Fosshage, J. L. (2000). The organizing functions of dreaming: A contemporary psychoanalytic model—Commentary on paper by Hazel Ipp. *Psychoanalytic Dialogues, 10,* 103–117.

Freud, S. (1894). The neuro-psychoses of defence. In J. Strachey (Ed. & Trans.), *The standard edition of the complete psychological works of Sigmund Freud* (Vol. 3, pp. 41–61). London: Hogarth Press.

Freud, S. (1896). Further remarks on the neuro-psychoses of defence. In J. Strachey (Ed. & Trans.), *The standard edition of the complete psychological works of Sigmund Freud* (Vol. 3, pp. 157–185). London: Hogarth Press.

Freud, S. (1905). Fragment of an analysis of a case of hysteria. In J. Strachey (Ed. & Trans.), *The standard edition of the complete psychological works of Sigmund Freud* (Vol. 7, pp. 1–122). London: Hogarth Press.

Freud, S. (1906). Letter from Sigmund Freud to C. G. Jung, December 6, 1906. *The Freud/Jung letters: The correspondence between Sigmund Freud and C. G. Jung.* Princeton, NJ: Princeton Univ. Press.

Freud, S. (1908). Creative writers and day-dreaming. In J. Strachey (Ed. & Trans.), *The standard edition of the complete psychological works of Sigmund Freud* (Vol. 9, pp. 141–154). London: Hogarth Press.

Freud, S. (1914). Remembering, repeating and working-through. In J. Strachey (Ed. & Trans.), *The standard edition of the complete psychological works of Sigmund Freud* (Vol. 12, pp. 145–156). London: Hogarth Press.

Freud, S. (1915a). The unconscious. In J. Strachey (Ed. & Trans.), *The standard edition of the complete psychological works of Sigmund Freud* (Vol. 14, pp. 159–215). London: Hogarth Press.

Freud, S. (1915b). Observations on transference-love. In J. Strachey (Ed. & Trans.), *The standard edition of the complete psychological works of Sigmund Freud* (Vol. 12, pp. 157–171). London: Hogarth Press.

Freud, S. (1918). From the history of an infantile neurosis. In J. Strachey (Ed. & Trans.), *The standard edition of the complete psychological works of Sigmund Freud* (Vol. 17, pp. 1–124). London: Hogarth Press.

Freud, S. (1920). Beyond the pleasure principle. In J. Strachey (Ed. & Trans.), *The standard edition of the complete psychological works of Sigmund Freud* (Vol. 18, pp. 1–64). London: Hogarth Press.

Freud, S., & Breuer, J. (1895). Preface to the first edition of *Studies on hysteria*. In J. Strachey (Ed. & Trans.), *The standard edition of the complete psychological works of Sigmund Freud* (Vol. 2, pp. xxix–xxx). London: Hogarth Press.

Gabbard, G. O. (2012). Deconstructing Vinculo. *Psychoanalytic Quarterly, 81,* 579–587.

Gentile, J. (2010). Weeds on the ruins: Agency, compromise formation, and the quest for intersubjective truth. *Psychoanalytic Dialogues, 20,* 88–109.

Ghent, E. (1990). Masochism, submission, surrender: Masochism as a perversion of surrender. *Contemporary Psychoanalysis, 26,* 108–136.

Ghent, E. (2002). Wish, need, drive. *Psychoanalytic Dialogues, 12,* 763–808.

Gill, M. M. (1983). The point of view of psychoanalysis: Energy discharge or person? *Psychoanalysis and Contemporary Thought, 6,* 523–551.

Grand, S. (2017). Seductive excess: Erotic transformations, secret predations. *Psychoanalytic Psychology, 34*, 208–214.

Greenberg, J. R. (1981). Prescription or description: The therapeutic action of psychoanalysis. *Contemporary Psychoanalysis, 17*, 239–257.

Greenberg, J. R. (1986). Theoretical models and the analyst's neutrality. *Contemporary Psychoanalysis, 22*, 87–106.

Greenberg, J. R. (2001). The analyst's participation. *Journal of the American Psychoanalytic Association, 49*, 359–381.

Grossmark, R. (2012). The flow of enactive engagement. *Contemporary Psychoanalysis, 48*, 287–300.

Grotstein, J. S. (2009). "The play's the thing wherein I'll catch the conscience of the king!" Psychoanalysis as a passion play. In: A. Ferro & R. Basile (Eds.), *The Analytic Field: A Clinical Concept*. London: Karnac.

Harris, A., & Aron, L. (1997). Ferenczi's semiotic theory: Previews of postmodernism. *Psychoanalytic Inquiry, 17*, 522–534.

Harris, A., Kalb, M., & Klebanoff, S. (2016a). *Ghosts in the consulting room*. London: Routledge.

Harris, A., Kalb, M., & Klebanoff, S. (2016b). *Demons in the consulting room*. London: Routledge.

Harris, A., & Kuchuck, S. (2015). *The legacy of Sándor Ferenczi: From ghost to ancestor*. London: Routledge.

Harris, A., & Sinsheimer, K. (2008). The analyst's vulnerability. In F. S. Anderson (Ed.), *Bodies in treatment: The unspoken dimension* (pp. 225–273). New York, NY: Routledge.

Hoffman, I. Z. (1983). The patient as interpreter of the analyst's experience. *Contemporary Psychoanalysis, 19*, 389–422.

Hoffman, I. Z. (2006). The myths of free association and the potentials of the analytic relationship. *International Journal of Psychoanalysis, 87*, 43–61.

Hoffman, M. T. (2011). *Toward mutual recognition: Relational psychoanalysis and the Christian narrative*. New York, NY: Routledge.

Hopkins, L., & Kuchuck, S. (Eds.) (in press). *Work books: The diaries of Masud Khan*. London: Routledge.

Jacoby, M. (1984). *The analytic encounter: Transference and human relationship*. Toronto: Inner City Books.

Jennings, S. (1997). *Introduction to dramatherapy: Theatre and healing—Ariadne's ball of thread*. London: Jessica Kingsley Publications.

Joseph, B. (1985). Transference: The total situation. *International Journal of Psychoanalysis, 66*, 447–454.

Jung, C. G. (1912). *Psychology of the unconscious: A study of the transformations and symbolisms of the libido. A contribution to the history of the evolution of thought.* Beatrice M. Hinkle, Trans (1916). London: Kegan Paul, Trench, Tubner (revised in 1952 as *Symbols of Transformation, Collected Works Vol. 5*).

Jung, C. G. (1916/1960). General aspects of dream psychology. In G. Adler & R. F. Hall (Eds. & Trans.), *Collected works* (Vol. 8, pp. 237–280). New York, NY: Pantheon.

Jung, C. G. (1961). *Memories, dreams, reflections.* New York, NY: Random House.

Jung, C. G. (1971). Psychological types. In *Collected works* (Vol. 6, pp. 3–555). London: Routledge & Kegan Paul.

Katz, G. (2013). *The play within the play: The enacted dimension of psychoanalytic process.* New York, NY: Routledge.

Katz, S. M. (2016). *Contemporary psychoanalytic field theory.* New York, NY: Routledge.

Kerr, J. (1993). *A most dangerous method: The story of Jung, Freud, and Sabina Spielrein.* New York, NY: Knopf.

Klein, M. (1946). Notes on some schizoid mechanisms. In *Envy and gratitude and other works, 1946–1963.* London: Hogarth Press, 1975, pp. 1–24.

Klein, M. (1955). On identification. In *Envy and gratitude and other works 1946–1963.* London, Hogarth Press, 1975, pp. 141–175.

Knoblauch, S. H. (2000). *The musical edge of therapeutic dialogue.* Hillsdale, NJ: The Analytic Press.

Kohut, H. (1971). *The analysis of the self.* New York, NY: International Universities Press.

Kristeva, J. (1982). *Powers of horror: An essay on abjection.* New York, NY: Columbia University Press.

Kuchuck, S. (2013). Reflections on the therapeutic action of desire. *Studies in Gender and Sexuality, 14*, 133–139.

Kuchuck, S. (2014). *Clinical implications of the psychoanalyst's life experience: When the personal becomes professional.* London: Routledge.

Kuchuck, S. (in press). On the limitations of love: Romance and loss in psychoanalysis. *Psychoanalytic Dialogues.*

Lacan, J. (1953/1956). The function and field of speech and language in psychoanalysis. In B. Fink (Trans.), *Écrits* (pp. 197–268). New York, NY: Norton.

Lachmann, F. M., & Lichtenberg, J. (1992). Model scenes: Implications for psychoanalytic treatment. *Journal of the American Psychoanalytic Association, 40,* 117–137.

Landy, R. J. (1986). *Drama therapy: Concepts, theories, and practices.* Springfield, IL: Charles Thomas.

Landy, R. J. (1993). *Persona and performance: The meaning of role in drama, therapy, and everyday life.* New York, NY: Guilford.

Langs, R., & Searles, H. F. (1980). *Intrapsychic and interpersonal dimensions of treatment: A clinical dialogue.* New York, NY: Jason Aronson.

Laplanche, J., & Pontalis, J. B. (1973). *The Language of Psychoanalysis.* New York, NY: W. W. Norton.

Lasky, R. (1993). *Dynamics of development and the therapeutic process.* Northvale, NJ: Jason Aronson.

Leavy, S. A. (1989). Time and world in the thought of Hans W. Loewald. *Psychoanalytic Study of the Child, 44,* 231–240.

Levenson, E. A. (1972). *The fallacy of understanding: An inquiry into the changing structure of psychoanalysis.* New York, NY: Basic Books.

Levenson, E. A. (1983). *The ambiguity of change: An inquiry into the nature of psychoanalytic reality.* New York, NY: Basic Books.

Levenson, E. A. (1985). The interpersonal (Sullivanian) model. In A. Rothstein (Ed.), *Models of the mind* (pp. 549–67). New York, NY: International Universities Press.

Lichtenberg, J., Lachmann, F., & Fosshage, J. (1996). *The clinical exchange: Techniques derived from self and motivational systems.* Hillsdale, NJ: The Analytic Press.

Loewald, H. W. (1962). The superego and the ego-ideal. *International Journal of Psychoanalysis, 43,* 264–268.

Loewald, H. W. (1979). The waning of the Oedipus complex. *Journal of the American Psychoanalytic Association, 27,* 751–775.

Lothane, Z. (2009). Dramatology in life, disorder, and psychoanalytic therapy: A further contribution to interpersonal psychoanalysis. *International Forum Psychoanalysis, 18*(3), 135–148.

Lothane, Z. (2010). Sándor Ferenczi, the dramatologist of love. *Psychoanalytic Perspectives, 7,* 165–182.

Lothane, Z. (2011). Dramatology vs. narratology: a new synthesis for psychiatry, psychoanalysis, and interpersonal drama therapy (IDT). *Archives of Psychiatry and Psychotherapy*, 2011; 4, 29–43.

McDougall, J. (1985[1982]). *Theaters of the mind: Illusion and truth on the psychoanalytic stage.* New York, NY: Basic Books.

McDougall, J. (1989). *Theaters of the body: A psychoanalytic approach to psychosomatic illness.* New York, NY: Norton.

Meltzer, D., & Williams, M. H. (1988). *The apprehension of beauty.* London: Karnac Books.

Miller, J. P. (1985). How Kohut actually worked. *Progress in Self Psychology, 1*, 13–30.

Mitchell, S. A. (1986). The wings of Icarus: Illusion and the problem of narcissism. *Contemporary Psychoanalysis, 22*, 107–132.

Mitchell, S. A. (1988). *Relational concepts in psychoanalysis.* Cambridge, MA: Harvard University Press.

Mitchell, S. A. (1991a). Wishes, needs and interpersonal negotiations. *Psychoanalytic Inquiry, 11*, 147–170.

Mitchell, S. A. (1991b). Contemporary perspectives on self: Toward an integration. *Psychoanalytic Dialogues, 1*, 121–147.

Mitchell, S. A. (1993). *Hope and dread in psychoanalysis.* New York, NY: Basic Books.

Mitchell, S. A. (1997). *Influence and autonomy in psychoanalysis.* Mahwah, NJ: Analytic Press.

Mitchell, S. A. (2000). *Relationality: From attachment to intersubjectivity.* Hillsdale, NJ: The Analytic Press.

Molino, A. (Ed.). (1996). *Elaborate selves.* New York, NY: Routledge.

Nelson, M. C., Nelson B., Sherman, M., & Strean, H. (1968). *Roles and paradigms in psychotherapy.* New York, NY: Grune & Stratton.

Ogden, T. H. (1979). On projective identification. *International Journal of Psychoanalysis, 60*, 357–373.

Ogden, T. H. (1994a). *Subjects of analysis.* Northvale, NJ: Jason Aronson.

Ogden, T. H. (1994b). The analytic third: Working with intersubjective clinical facts. *International Journal of Psychoanalysis, 75*, 3–19.

Ogden, T. H. (2005). *This art of psychoanalysis: Dreaming undreamt dreams and interrupted cries.* London: Routledge.

Ogden, T. H. (2007a). Reading Harold Searles. *International Journal of Psychoanalysis, 88*, 353–369.

Ogden, T. H. (2007b). On talking-as-dreaming. *International Journal of Psychoanalysis, 88*, 575–589.

Ogden, T. H. (2015). Intuiting the truth of what's happening: On Bion's "Notes on memory and desire." *Psychoanalytic Quarterly, 84*, 285–306.

Orange, D. M. (2011). *The suffering stranger: Hermeneutics for everyday clinical practice.* New York, NY: Routledge.

Ornstein, A. (1974). The dread to repeat and the new beginning. *Annual of Psychoanalysis, 2*, 231–248.

Person, E. S. (1995). *By force of fantasy: How we make our lives.* New York, NY: Basic Books.

Pollock, L., & Slavin, J. H. (1998). The struggle for recognition: Disruption and reintegration in the experience of agency. *Psychoanalytic Dialogues, 8*, 857–873.

Razinsky, L. (2013). *Freud, psychoanalysis and death.* Cambridge: Cambridge University Press.

Ricoeur, P. (1970). *Freud and philosophy* (D. Savage, Trans.). New Haven, CT: Yale University Press.

Ringstrom, P. A. (2001). Cultivating the improvisational in psychoanalytic treatment. *Psychoanalytic Dialogues, 11*, 727–754.

Roth, M. (2017). *Reading the Reader: A Psychoanalytic Perspective on Reading Literature.* In Hebrew: (Eds.) Avi Sagi & Aner Govrin, Psychoanalysis, Hermeneutics and Culture Book Series. Jerusalem: Carmel.

Roth, M. (in press). True love as the love of truth: A Kleinian take on romantic love. *Psychoanalytic Perspectives.*

Salberg, J. (2010). *Good enough endings: Breaks, interruptions, and terminations from contemporary relational perspectives.* New York, NY: Routledge.

Samuels, A. (1985). *Jung and the post-Jungians.* London: Routledge.

Sandler, J. (1976). Countertransference and role-responsiveness. *International Review of Psychoanalysis, 3*, 43–47.

Sawyer, A. (2011). Let's talk: A narrative of mental illness, recovery, and the psychotherapist's personal treatment. *Journal of Clinical Psychology: In Session, 67*(8), 776–788.

Sawyer, A. (2013). "Is diagnosis destiny?" Presented at the 9th Annual Yale NEA–BPD Conference, May 10, 2013, Yale University School of Medicine, New Haven, CT. Available as a YouTube Video: www.youtube.com/watch?v=Wt_h0Ro26Lw

Schafer, R. (1976). *A new language for psychoanalysis*. New Haven, CT: Yale University Press.

Schafer, R. (1983). *The analytic attitude*. New York, NY: Basic Books.

Searles, H. F. (1960). *The nonhuman environment: In normal development and in schizophrenia*. Madison, CT: International Universities Press.

Searles, H. F. (1965). *Collected papers on schizophrenia and related subjects*. Madison, CT: International Universities Press.

Searles, H. F. (1968–1969). Roles and paradigms in psychotherapy. *Psychoanalytic Review, 55*, 697–700.

Searles, H. F. (1975). The patient as therapist to his analyst. In P. Giovacchini (Ed.), *Tactics and techniques in psychoanalytic therapy* (pp. 95–151). New York, NY: Jason Aronson.

Searles, H. F. (1979). *Countertransference and related subjects: Selected papers*. New York, NY: International Universities Press.

Searles, H. F. (1986). *My work with borderline patients*. Northvale, NJ: Jason Aronson.

Sedgwick, D. (1993). *Jung and Searles*. London: Routledge.

Semetsky, I. (2013). *Jung and educational theory*. Hoboken, NJ: Wiley-Blackwell.

Severn, E. (1933/2017). *The discovery of the self*. London: Routledge.

Slavin, J. H. (2007). The imprisonment and liberation of love: The dangers and possibilities of love in the psychoanalytic relationship. *Psychoanalytic Inquiry, 27*, 197–218.

Slavin, J. H., & Rahmani, M. (2015). The legitimate guiding forces of one's behavior in the world: Discussion of "Generative enactment: Memories from the future" by Aron and Atlas. *Psychoanalytic Dialogues, 25*, 325–334.

Slavin, J. & Rahmani, M. (2016). Slow dancing: Mind, body, and sexuality in a new relational psychoanalysis. *Psychoanalytic Perspectives, 13*, 152–167.

Slavin, M. O., & Kriegman, D. (1998). Why the analyst needs to change: Toward a theory of conflict, negotiation, and mutual influence in the therapeutic process. *Psychoanalytic Dialogues, 8*, 247–284.

Soloveitchik, J. B. (2000). *Fate and destiny: From Holocaust to the State of Israel* (L. Kaplan, Trans.). Hoboken, NJ: KTAV Publishing.

Spotnitz, H. (1969). *Modern psychoanalysis of the schizophrenic patient*. New York, NY: Grune and Stratton.

Stanislavski, C. (1936). *An actor prepares* (Elizabeth Hapgood, Trans.). New York, NY: Theatre Arts Books.

Stern, D. B. (1997). *Unformulated experience: From dissociation to imagination in psychoanalysis*. Hillsdale, NJ: The Analytic Press.

Stern, D. B. (2004). The eye sees itself. *Contemporary Psychoanalysis, 40*, 197–237.

Stern, D. B. (2013). Relational freedom and therapeutic action. *Journal of the American Psychoanalytic Association, 61*, 227–256.

Stern, D. B. (2015). *Relational freedom: Emergent properties of the interpersonal field*. London: Routledge.

Stern, S. (1994). Needed relationships and repeated relationships: An integrated relational perspective. *Psychoanalytic Dialogues, 4*, 317–346.

Stern, S. (2002). The self as a relational structure: A dialogue with multiple-self theory. *Psychoanalytic Dialogues, 12*, 693–714.

Stern, S. (2017). *Needed relationships and psychoanalytic healing*. New York, NY: Routledge.

Suchet, M. (2016). Surrender, transformation, and transcendence. *Psychoanalytic Dialogues, 26*, 747–760.

Sullivan, H. (1953). *The interpersonal theory of psychiatry*. New York, NY: Norton.

Tolpin, M. (2002). Doing psychoanalysis of normal development. *Progress in Self Psychology, 18*, 167–190.

Wangh, M. (1962). The "evocation of a proxy": A psychological maneuver, its use as a defense, its purpose and genesis. *Psychoanalytic Study of the Child, 17*, 451–469.

Winnicott, D. W. (1971). *Playing and reality*. London: Tavistock Publications.

Index